Je T'aime

"Everyone can say it right . . .
no one says it like you."

A love story of loss,
heartbreak, and renewal.

Nicole Leclerc Cunningham

Je T'aime

Published by:

Peak Publishing • Denver, CO 80219
(Division of: www.healthylifepress.com)

Author: Nicole Leclerc Cunningham
Illustrator: Sharon Reeves
Designer: Judy Johnson

Printed in the United States of America

Library of Congress Cataloging-in-Publication Data
Cunningham, Nicole Leclerc
Je T'aime

ISBN **978-1-547218-59-2**
1. RELIGION / Christian Life/Death, Grief, Bereavement
2. SELF-HELP / Death, Grief, Bereavement

Most Healthy Life Press resources are available wherever books are sold. Distribution is primarily through *Amazon.com* and *healthylifepress.com*. Multiple copy discounts are available directly from Healthy Life Press. Wholesale distribution of this book is exclusively through *CreateSpace.com*. Contact the publisher if you have questions about how to obtain a retailer's discount. Epublications of this book are available only through *Amazon.com* (KDP)—for all eBook readers—or by request from the publisher (*info@healthylifepress.com*).

Back cover photo of the author is courtesy of Life Touch Church Directories and Portraits.

Acknowledgements

Bob Muntz
for his support and guidance
that led to the publishing of this book.

Dr. Larry Smith
for his encouraging word
after reviewing excerpts of the manuscript.

Eric Ebinger
author, editor, for the energy and enthusiasm he
brought to our meetings and for making the book a reality.

Sharon Reeves
for the beautiful art work and for
the friendship we have shared through many years.

Daughter Jessica
for sharing much of my incredible journey
and for her constant love, support, and encouragement.

Dr. David Biebel, Publisher,
for his uncanny ability to relate to the heart of the book
from the start and for making this process an enjoyable journey.

Judy Johnson, Designer,
for her remarkable talent that
made the book aesthetically delightful.

Dedication

to John
my best friend and soul-mate.

to Jessica
"ma Raison d'Etre".

to Ian and Owen
"ma Joie de Vivre".

to Cory
for his steadfast love.

to our wonderful friends
for their love and support.

Introduction

Grief—I had studied it, attended grief seminars, and had become very familiar with the stages one must go through to find solace and peace. In my profession, I had often helped terminally ill patients die a more peaceful death while helping families through their grief. I thought I knew my stuff. Then Johnny died. . . .

I was twenty-eight and had recently left a marriage consumed by alcoholism when I was introduced to John, a tall, handsome, fifty-year-old bearded man who had lived the bachelor life for almost a decade . . . and he did not drink. John had been sober twenty-five years and had quit for the same reason he quit boxing in his college years: "The referee kept stepping on my hands," he would say. Pain, the great motivator!

At John's request, a mutual friend had introduced us. Years later, in his unique sense of humor, John would refer to our friend and say: "He introduced me to my wife and I have not spoken to him since. . . ." A week after our first encounter, when he had finally found a way to contact me and I did not remember who he was, John sarcastically said: "I made a hell of an impression on you, didn't I!" From that day forward we would become good friends, eventually lovers, partners in marriage, best friends, and soulmates, a thirty-two-year journey that would remain alive and vibrant through death and beyond.

There is no chronological order or succession of events in my relating what I have lived after John's passing. I just knew that it was all too big to keep inside and felt like I would run out of space in my heart and soul. As I lived each experience, there was this strong urge to write, sometimes talking directly to Johnny and at other times describing what I was living. Each event was written as it happened, wherever I happened to be, on whatever piece of paper I could find, the words pouring out of me until it was finished. Through each one, it was as if writing about it lessened the intensity and the fullness inside my whole being. During those first years of mourning, often just going through the motion of living, time was non-existent. Only love and sorrow propelled my entire being until healing came, at its own time, in its own way.

1

I watched the last breath of life moving out of your body and felt the most excruciating pain, like a knife had gone through my chest and ripped my heart open. I had never known such pain. . . . I didn't know it existed. All I wanted was for you to take me with you. In that heart-wrenching moment, I could not have known that love would not only live on, but would intensify as it transformed itself into something I could not have fathomed. I could not have known that I would live this incredible journey, filled with the most intense pain, delirious encounters, visions of a mystical nature, out-of-body experiences, love beyond measure, all-encompassing joy, and through it all, gratitude that would fill every space in my wounded soul.

Grief is often viewed as a wound, an emptiness in the pit of the stomach, a process you need to get through to go on with your life. I am not "going through" grief. I am living grief every day since Johnny passed on—a mélange of the deepest pain, the greatest joy, being fully aware, fully alive, allowing what is evolving inside me to come to life in its own time, in its own way, wherever I am and for whatever time it needs to be lived and understood. At times, the pain is almost unbearable. At times, the desire to go on leaves. At times, I can't make sense of anything in my life. Often, I feel his presence, I see his shadow, I hear his voice and his words clearly spoken. Sitting on the swing, where time often eluded us, I feel the sadness that often turns into despair deep in my soul as the tears flow.

Sometimes I get a glimpse of hope like a minute spark of light in the depth of my being. I cannot think of tomorrow. I can only stay in this moment. There is no emptiness in the pit of my stomach; sitting here alone with my thoughts, even through the intense pain I always feel gratitude for what has been and for what remains. It is often too big for me to understand and to take in. There are always tears, unending tears. Sometimes they fall softly down my cheeks. At other times, they well up inside me until I feel like I am going to burst and then I sob and for a little while feel the hopelessness. . . . Yet, through it all, I wouldn't change a thing. This is my life today.

At one time in our life, there seemed to be so little time. I used to "stretch" the week-ends by attempting to live each moment as completely as I could. Now, I find myself sitting alone at the table by the picture window, reading a few uplifting messages and then staring at the huge Sycamore tree—the little stick our young daughter brought home from kindergarten—sometimes for what seems like a few minutes and at other times like hours. I never really know. Sitting there, I often feel your presence and it brings me peace and comfort.

Spring came, my first spring without Johnny. It felt like the cold of winter remained frozen in my heart and soul. Trees all around the land were showing signs of life as new leaves sprung on bare branches, except for the Sycamore in the middle of the field.

That Sycamore tree looked like it was dying; the new leaves were brown and dried up quickly. The man who mowed our lawn for years confirmed that the tree was dead. . . . I couldn't take it! That tree was alive because of John. I couldn't bear the thought of losing it, not now. I remember walking to the tree, my eyes filled with tears. I began stroking the bark on the huge trunk while caressing some of the branches, talking to it and begging that it would live. Within a few weeks, to my amazement, the Sycamore grew new leaves, green and healthy. I thanked the tree, John, and God—in that order.

I have been praying to feel joy again. I feel like my joy died with John. Early on the day he crossed over, I told him to please ask God to save me a place beside him. A few hours later I was holding him when he took his last breath. . . . How I wanted to die with him. I kissed his lips and they were cold. I remember sobbing and trembling and telling him that I loved him. I held on to his hand and kept it warm until they came for him. Our friends gathered around the bed and recited the Lord's Prayer. I felt no comfort, just excruciating pain.

When they came for him, I slowly let go of his hand and walked away to the kitchen. As I stood beside my friend something incredible happened! I felt John's arms around me, holding me.... There he stood, tall and strong, the way he used to be. I told my friend: "John is here." She nodded and I realized that she knew. After they dressed him in one of his favorite outfits I touched his body from head to toe for the last time and took off the ring that had never left his finger for thirty years. And then, they took him away. My good friend, who has stood by me ever since, took the ring from my hand and put it, with the small cross, on the chain around my neck. It is still there to this day.

It had been a hard, cold winter and I now felt cold all the way inside my being. Even under a hot shower, I couldn't feel warm for a long, long time. At first, he came to me in my dreams, and then he just came to me. I didn't feel so cold anymore. Sometimes I even felt a ray of warmth enveloping my whole being. I was grateful.

For months, I kept the lights low and the sounds in the house barely audible. I felt like the whole world was at a standstill, like nothing moved except the wrenching pain inside me ravaging the very core of my being. For the first month and a half, friends streamed in and out every single day but two. They asked and I told, reliving on the outside what was tearing me apart inside. They cared enough to listen. They read the articles in the newspapers. They cried with me and laughed with me. They loved him, too. They would miss him. Their visits did not take the pain away, but they brought hope and comfort and that was enough.

We had gotten Nigel, our Chow, as a young puppy and he was now three. Johnny would often refer to him as my dog, especially as his illness progressed. As the shadow of death hovered over the hospital bed, Nigel refused to come in the house until what would be the last day. He walked straight to the bed, put his chin by Johnny's face for a moment, walked all around the bed, went back outside and would not come back in.

Somehow, he knew your time had come. At nine forty-five, with my arms around you, you passed on. Now Nigel walks to where your bed stood and whines and cries for you . . . and I cry with him as I tell him, "From now on it's just the two of us."

I am so grateful that you chose him for us, for me. How was it, now? After you had already chosen him, you asked if I would like to go see a puppy. I remember on the way home you asked me, "Do you want him?"

"It's okay with me," I answered. "That's not the answer I want," you said, a big grin on your face. I finally said, "Sure, I want him." The next day I came home from work to Nigel, our Chow. I still wasn't quite sure how it had happened, but we both grew to love him and he continues to bring me comfort and joy. He is really "my" dog, and we both love you so.

Nigel would mourn Johnny with me for years to come.

When Johnny died, I had questions that weighed heavily on my heart and burst out of me. I needed to know, from this God I believed in:

"Who are you?"

"What are you?"

"Where is John?"

"What happened to his spirit?"

"What about the life he just left? Does he know?"

"Will he know me? Or me, him?"

I felt desperate. I needed answers. My God had mercy on me. I got answers . . . in ways I couldn't have imagined . . . through reading his Word, people put in my path at just the right time, books written in different languages recounting similar experiences of the Other Side, insightful readings on the afterlife and mostly, personal experiences beyond anything my mind could have conceived, and incidents that were at times witnessed by friends that were beyond anything that could be rationally explained but could not be denied. Through it all, I kept on learning, discovering, and understanding a little more with each passing day.

I have no doubt today: John has found healing and peace with God. I also know in the depth of my being that love never dies. John is with me even when I release him to his new life on the Other Side. I see his "shadow" and I cannot change what he is wearing, usually clothing from when he was healthy and strong. I hear his voice, and his messages come when I need them the most. I feel his presence and sometimes his touch. He also comes in my dreams, strong and vibrant. At times, he lets me know he is around in ways that he only could imagine. At such times, I can see his big grin when I finally realize what is happening. I pray to feel joy again. In these special times, he brings joy back in my life and makes me smile through my tears.

When I get up in the morning and walk to the window, I am always so touched when there is a warm, bright sun. The song "On Eagle's Wings," by Michael Joncas, always comes to mind. This is the song we chose to end the celebration of John's life. When John was at the Rehab Center for a whole month, I would kneel by our bed every night and I would always see him in his navy and green plaid pajamas curled up in God's hand. After Johnny died, the first morning I opened the drapes to a bright sunrise, I saw him standing triumphant in God's hand, with his arms stretched upward toward the sun. The vision filled my whole being with an overwhelming feeling of joy! How comforting. . . . Now, when I open the drapes to a bright, sunny morning, I often have this incredible, beautiful vision of the two of us standing in God's hand with our arms around each other. Such a heartwarming sight!

Sometime after Johnny died, I opened the top drawer of his dresser and just looked. There were his handkerchiefs, boxer shorts, and T-shirts folded in a high pile (after he retired and took over the laundry), and then his wallet holding a few pictures, his social security, Medicare, and insurance cards, all the things that defined his existence in the eyes of society . . . in a breath made inconsequential, like the world saying: "Yesterday you were someone, but today you do not exist anymore." It all seemed so cruel. I stood there, tears flowing at first softly and then sobbing uncontrollably until I was completely exhausted—another night with no respite for my troubled soul.

For days and weeks and months after you passed on to the Other Side, I felt cold, chilled to the bones. Nothing could warm my trembling body, what felt like cold blood coursed through my veins and my aching heart. How I yearned for your embrace and your warmth. Spring came. On a crisp morning as I was walking along our small country road with our dog I could feel the rays from the bright sun reach way deep inside me. I felt warm all over for the first time in a long, long time . . . and there you were, walking beside me, olive green jacket with brown suede collar, red knitted hat, gray sweats, tennis shoes, and a big grin on your face. I'll take you any way you come, Johnny.

One beautiful summer day, a friend came to visit, bring-

ing a wonderful lunch in her basket. "Why don't we eat out on the swing?" she proposed. I felt my throat tightening, but did not say anything as we walked out to the swing a few minutes later. For the first time, someone else would sit in your place, on the swing. I was telling myself it would be okay, but I wasn't sure how. We ate and talked and ate. Later, I thanked her. She didn't realize the healing gift her presence on the swing had been. Such a small step and yet so big! Life does go on.

The two crab apple trees we planted together a few years ago had only a few blossoms each year. Every time we walked around "the plantation"—as you so often referred to our land—I would touch their branches and marvel at their beauty. But this year, for the first time, each branch is filled with blossoms . . . like they are celebrating life, your life. They are magnificent! They bring me hope and joy.

A few weeks ago, during a telephone conversation with our daughter Jessica, she exclaimed: "Mom you're really laughing, all the way from your toes!" The thought that I could laugh again was exhilarating! The other day she was here and we laughed so hard, we were both crying. What a blessing!

As I write this, he is seven years old—the grandchild his mother refers to as "an old soul." He is insightful—a beautiful, gentle soul. He is also stubborn and determined once he makes up his mind about something. One night, he was in his bedroom getting ready for bed. He had just gotten a new dresser and earlier that day he had reached up on a shelf and taken down a picture in a small frame and placed it on his new dresser. On the picture, he was sitting on his Grandpapa's lap on the swing and beside them his little brother is sitting on Grandmaman's lap.

He had taken the picture in his hands, stared at it for a short time and then begun to cry. By the time his mother walked in to tuck him in bed he was sobbing. She asked why he was so sad and he told her that he was remembering how happy his Grandmaman was when Grandpapa was with her. He then added that he had remembered Grandpapa's story about being in the army and had saluted his photograph.

"Wrong hand, Ian," he had heard Grandpapa's voice say. Ian is left-handed and Grandpapa had told him once that you always salute with your right hand. He had forgotten and Grandpapa had reminded him. His mom cried with him. He could not fall asleep. Later that night he called and related what had happened, crying, filled with emotions, and missing his Grandpapa. I cried with him and reminded him how special he was and how much his Grandpapa loved him and was watching over him. After a while, I reminded him of all the times he had asked Grandpapa, "Can I ride your chair?"

"Only one time," he would answer. And the lift-chair would go up and down and up and down . . . He laughed. We hung up and he went to sleep.

I am looking at the flowers coming to life by the swing. They were planted last spring, a few months after Johnny died. They had been sent to honor him and I wanted them by the swing, our special place. We would work outside on "the plantation," sometimes until we were exhausted and hungry. Then we would sit on the swing and catch our breath . . . for a few minutes or for what seemed like eternity. We would sit, at times silent, the swing barely moving, looking, smelling, listening, feeling. We would have snacks of cheese, crackers, and salami. He would drink his favorite drink of tonic water and lime and I would quench my thirst with whatever suited my fancy. It is there on the swing, the last summer when the illness took over our lives, that the words were spoken—we would always meet on the swing. I cried. He was sad. We both knew there might not be another summer. There wasn't. I planted the flowers the following spring. That was one year ago. Not one flower bloomed that summer. It felt like death was still hovering over the swing. But this year, they are red, yellow, and pure white. I don't know their names and it doesn't matter. I love looking at them, smelling them, touching them. They bring me joy and for a while I feel alive again.

I needed to touch you, to rub your hand, to feel your warmth. How I miss you. That night you came to me in a dream. I was in a large pool and there were a lot of creatures, big and small. Somehow, I did not feel threatened by them. I was not afraid. As I walked toward the shallow end, the creatures diminished in size until they disappeared. You came in the water, took me in your arms and carried me out. My yellow and cream striped robe covered my body. There were a lot of people looking at us. You didn't seem to care. You looked at me with that loving look in your eyes. You carried me proudly. Your arms were strong and you stood tall. How I love you.

I was sobbing. I said that you could go. I wanted you to be free to experience life on the Other Side the way you were meant to, without worrying about me. It was heart-wrenching, but I knew I had to release you so you could begin your journey to the Supreme Being.

I cried myself to sleep. In the morning, I went outside and sat on the swing. I immediately felt his presence beside me. There he sat in his plaid polo shirt and olive green shorts. We were silent. After a while he got up from the swing. I followed him. We began walking "around the plantation" like we always did, looking at every tree, me touching their branches, leaves, and needles. We walked quietly, side by side. As I got to the end of our walk, I was alone. I felt sad but so grateful.

He loved all of me. I felt so accepted by him, so fulfilled, and so loved. He believed in me, stood by me, and was proud to refer to me as "my bride." People who first met us often thought we were newlyweds . . . thirty years later. He would often say, "You're a genius," when I figured out something rather simple or fixed an appliance or got a tool to work. Far from the truth as it was, that little phrase meant the world to me. I often hear those words still. . . . Our relationship was far from perfect, but it was real, strong, loyal, and so warm and comfortable. A very good friend said: "The relationship was not perfect, but the love was." How profound! It was everything and still is. I loved all of him. I still do.

I felt loss. The one person in this world who loved and accepted all of me was gone. I felt like hiding from the world, literally. How was it possible that life went on as usual while my whole world had just been shattered to pieces? I let everything grow wild on our land . . . bushes with weeds growing in between, cotton trees planted by the birds and the wind sprouted everywhere, and wherever an opening let the outside world peak in, I transplanted more bushes, all to hide from the living.

But today I am opening myself to life—overgrown shrubs are being trimmed or cut down, weeds are pulled and the grass is cut. Today, I am letting the sun shine through and I am welcoming the outside world into my world. Today, my inside and my outside are more in sync and I am in the world of the living.

2

He had an incredible mind, ingenious, creative, and imaginative. He had a passion for history, especially the Civil War and World War II. He loved books and owned many of the great classics. He could recite pages and pages of Shakespeare and everyone would marvel at his ability to recite a poem about any subject being brought up. When he became ill with Parkinson's disease, he memorized and recited "Casey at the Bat" to the amusement of our friends who never seemed to tire of listening to him. His mind never failed him or others until the very end.

Someone said to me that I would momentarily mistake someone for Johnny, something I knew in my heart to be impossible until that one day. I was leaving work when my eye caught a glimpse of a tall, gray-haired gentleman wearing a pink polo shirt, light gray pants, and tan suede shoes, with the same demeanor as Johnny as he turned the corner of the building and disappeared. For that split second it was Johnny . . . the hair, the clothes, the walk . . . before I knew it, I could barely see for the tears running down my face. I ran to my car and sobbed.

During a staff meeting, there was a demonstration on the newest equipment for delivering oxygen to a patient. The swishing sound of the machine immediately brought me back to John's side, my one hand around his head, holding his hand with the other, talking to him, watching, waiting, crying, with the constant, unsettling swishing sound in the background. After a few minutes, I was so filled with emotions I felt like my chest was going to burst open. I ran out of the room crying and babbling: "I need to get out of here." The next day, a picture of the two of us sat on my desk, something to bring me back to life, to love. . . .

Much later, I was at a luncheon with a group of women, some married, others widowed or single. We were laughing at each other's jokes. Sex came up, as it seems to with joke telling. "I don't miss it," a widow said. "I don't, either," replied another. I was silent. I missed him so.

I missed all of him, his handsome body even as it became thinner and frail, his great mind, and his beautiful soul. I missed his sense of humor, his intense, often uptight ways. I missed enjoying a gourmet meal or a hot dog with him. I missed touching him, caressing his hand, making love with him. I missed walking around "the plantation" with him, sitting on the swing, gardening, pulling weeds, and walking in the rain. I missed curling up with him at night, his one arm around my neck and the other wrapped around my waist, our bodies molded into each other. I missed the way he would turn the sound off during commercials while he did the commercials himself with a big grin on his face. I missed fighting over his refusal to change his sweats with a stain at the wrong spot. I missed his lips, running my hand through his hair, cuddling up on the La-Z-Boy, breathing with him. I missed listening to the poems about "the morn, in russet mantle clad. . . ." life, death, Hamlet, Macbeth. I missed . . . I missed . . . I missed all of him.

3

I got up late. I had been up late the night before looking at pictures, talking to God and to John, releasing him once more through my unending tears. I finally felt a sense of peace and tranquility and went to sleep. The morning was bright with the sun shining high. I walked into the sunroom as I did every morning. It is a peaceful room where nature reaches inside. I looked around and felt joy well up inside me.

Joy . . . what I had been praying for and now it felt alive again. For the longest time, it seemed like my joy had died with John, like I had dried up inside. I glanced through the

sliding doors at the birdbath, my eyes moving to the Snow Fountains Weeping Cherry tree where John's ashes had been laid to rest. It was then that I noticed, at the bottom of the tree, that the stone that had been placed atop the ashes appeared to be standing on its side. Convinced that this could not be, I left the room, a heavy feeling welling up in my chest. *I am not seeing right*, I thought. I walked back to the bedroom, brushed my teeth, and put on a shirt and shoes.

I went back into the sunroom, expecting to find things the way they had been the night before. To my disbelief, the stone *was* standing. I nervously opened the sliding doors and walked to the tree. The stone was up, resting on the stick supporting the newly planted tree. I sat down in the grass and looked . . . and looked . . . tears flowing down my cheeks. The dirt under the stone was slightly disturbed, exposing some of the ashes. I ran my fingers lightly on the ashes, John's ashes.

A few roots were exposed, the same way they had been when I had dug the hole before the "Ceremony of Burial of the Ashes." I looked carefully, trying to understand how this could be. The ground around the stone had not been disturbed, except for the little dirt "brushed aside" under the stone, exposing ashes. *There is an explanation*, I thought . . . a wild animal, a dog maybe . . . but there were no marks on the ground around the tree. Over an acre of land, and this very spot only had been disturbed. There was no way to explain the stone raised up and leaning neatly against the stick, the dirt moved slightly under the stone only. *Was I*

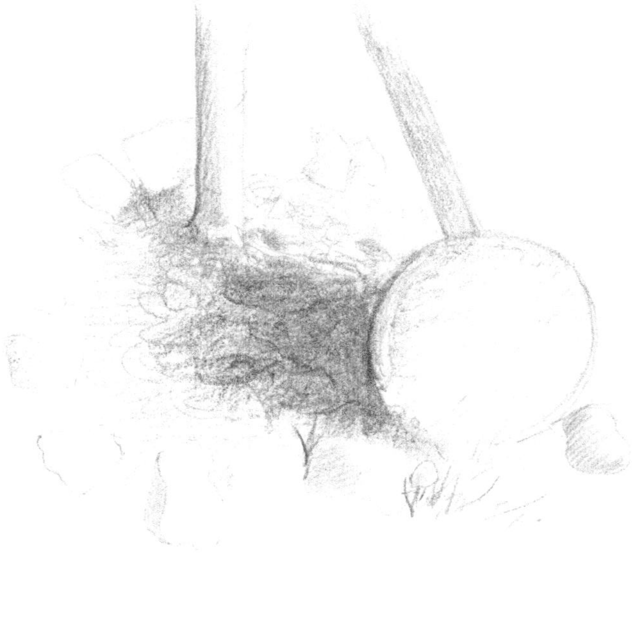

really seeing this, experiencing this? I needed confirmation. I called our very good friends and simply muttered through tears, "The stone is raised. . . ." *An engineer will find an explanation*, I thought. They came, looked, and found no plausible explanation. They took turns praying as we held hands around the tree. Something big had taken place, almost too big for me to fathom.

The stone was moved, the ashes exposed to the warm rays of the sun. There was a sense of freedom, of sacredness. I knelt and slowly brushed the dirt with my fingers and covered the ashes. I placed the round, heavy stone back on top. I felt John's presence. I turned and watched as he ran in the grass toward the sun. We were both free in that incredible moment!

4

The boys, then five and seven, were visiting for the weekend. As usual, the three of us slept on the sofa bed in the den. First, we had popcorn and pop while watching "Beethoven," the movie about the St. Bernard. We laughed a lot, yelled a little, said our prayers, and then Ian and I told each other stories while his little brother slept, his head at the foot of the sofa bed. The next morning as we were folding in the sofa bed Ian exclaimed: "Look!" He was glancing between the back of the sofa and the mattress. "Looks like dog food back there. . . ."

It was! I immediately wanted to know

who, when, and how as I scolded and demanded the truth. I was very upset and wanted an answer. Little Owen was crying as he confessed that maybe he had done it and had forgotten. He could not explain how or when and I couldn't either. Then Ian confessed, saying, "I think maybe I did it." But he could not explain it, either. It was so neatly done. Besides, the children had not been alone while unfolding the sofa bed and the fifty pounds of dog food was kept in a large metal can in the garage.

Nothing made sense to me. Then I remembered a similar incident. A few weeks prior, I had found dog food strung neatly against the wall at the back of a closet I had cleaned and reorganized just days before. I had immediately picked up the pieces, one by one, and dismissed the incident—out of sight, out of mind—but now it all came back to me. I had cleaned and rearranged the closet and had placed a braided rug at the bottom for shoes and boots. And then dog food? No one else was around but me. How could I have put it out of my mind so easily??? I began to wonder. . . .

Was it you both times? In your usual "twisted" sense of humor you knew I would blame it on the children and then realize that they could not have done it. They did not have the opportunity and both had confessed to "cover up" for the other. In my mind's eye, I immediately saw your big grin and I knew. . . . I had been praying to feel joy inside instead of deep sorrow whenever I felt your presence. I began to laugh . . . hysterically . . . I love you so.

A few days later, Ian admitted to making up a story to save his little brother. Neither one had done it. Of that I was certain. I reminded them that all I expected was the truth. They didn't ask for an explanation and I didn't think it necessary.

I have laughed about that incident many times since, picturing your crooked smile that said: "I made you laugh didn't I!" Thank you, Johnny, for bringing laughter back into my life.

5

Many people attended the mass in celebration of John's life. The funeral director asked if I would stand at the back of the church to greet them. I knew I couldn't do it. I didn't have the strength. One by one they marched down to the first pew. They kept coming, a procession of love, hugs, kind words, and many tears. I remember saying that I didn't know how to live without John. It was like the raw, intense pain engulfing my insides left no space for life to go on. Mass started. "Dad's here. . . ." I said quietly to our daughter as I moved closer to her to make room for him in the pew, "and he's wearing shorts." We would argue over his wanting to wear shorts to church. "It's not respectful," I would say. He had that grin that said: "I'm here in my shorts to be with you." Today, I will have him any way he comes.

We both had willed our bodies to the Medical College of Ohio early on in our marriage. After they took John, they told me it could take up to a year to get his ashes. One day in early December, I was sitting at the table looking out at the bare Sycamore. It was a cold morning. The first Cardinal appeared and perched itself on the bush by the side window. John loved watching birds and he especially loved Cardinals. There was something comforting watching the first bright red bird of the season. A few moments later I heard the "beep" outside. I had to sign for a letter. My hands were shaking and tears silently flooded my eyes, cold drops wetting my cheeks. I could not look up. The letter was from MCO. Nine months later. I walked back into the house and sat down, immobilized, the letter in front of me. I could not bring myself to open it. Not now. I looked for the December issue of "Daily Word" for comfort and was greeted by a beautiful red Cardinal on the cover. "Thank you," I muttered. I knew it was going to be okay. When we picked up the ashes, a few days later, I couldn't say a word, not even my name. Our daughter was my angel. When we got back in the car, she handed me the box. We opened it together, looked and wept silently. Then it happened . . . we both felt his presence strongly. Again, I knew it was going to be okay.

When I got home from MCO, I placed the small box containing John's ashes on the dresser by our bed. Every night, I opened the box, undid the tie, and looked at the ashes. It was hard to believe that the hands I loved to caress and hold, even until after he took his last breath, were now ashes. I cried and prayed and cried. Night after night. Nothing made sense, and I couldn't make sense of anything. *How can my lover, my best friend, my soulmate be ashes?* I wondered. I would imagine his blue eyes looking deeply into mine for the last time, his lips, his hands, his touch, how I needed him and wanted him. And then he would be there ... his presence felt intensely. Even now, it feels like my heart is not big enough to hold all the pain.

I miss you Johnny. Je t'aime.

John and I had decided that we wanted our ashes buried on our land. We would put his ashes in the ground early in January so family, a few friends, and our priest, could attend. December ended up being very cold. The ground was frozen solid. Late that month I went outside early in the morning, a small shovel in my hand, to dig three small holes, one under the big Maple tree John had transplanted about ten years earlier. "Come and see what I did!" he had said proudly. The tree was already over ten feet tall and was leaning on one side. He had a board leaning against the tree and told me it would straighten itself up. I didn't really believe it would. It did. Today it stands at least forty feet tall, strong, straight, and beautiful. "Just like John did for many people," our priest would say during the blessing of ashes. I knelt and started digging close to the tree. My tears felt cold on my cheeks and I could barely see, but I was able to break through the frozen ground and make a small hole. I got up and felt a presence, John's presence. We walked silently side-by-side toward the next tree, the huge Sycamore.

In kindergarten, our daughter had come home with a little stick that John had planted in the middle of the field. Grandpa (honorary title for our special neighbor) had mowed the field with his big tractor. The little stick was gone. She was in tears. John dug out the roots and planted them in front of the big window. It is the biggest tree on our land today. As we got closer to the Sycamore, John stopped and stood a few feet from the tree, as if to wait for me. I got closer, got down on my knees and began to dig, but I couldn't break the frozen ground. I looked up and with a glance John showed me where the ground was softer and I dug the hole. He was still standing there when I got up. We walked together toward the third tree, a small Snow Fountains Weeping Cherry we had planted the previous April in his memory. At the foot of the tree stands a bronze eagle with the flag donated by the Veterans of World War II. I knelt by the tree. I was alone again. The digging was easy. But doing it was so painful. I couldn't stop the tears. I walked back to each tree and covered the holes with a small board in case of another snowstorm. I walked away feeling cold all the way inside.

In January, family and friends gathered for the "Ceremony of Burial of the Ashes." As we gathered around each tree, our priest, a longtime friend, read from The Book held by a grandchild while the younger child spread incense. After the prayers, our priest asked that I place some of John's ashes in each person's hand so they could deposit them in each hole before I covered them with dirt. The box and bag were burnt by the last tree. Ashes to ashes. . . .

I couldn't wash my hand that whole day and night. Even as I write about it, it is hard to describe the emotions that overtook me as my hand held the ashes of my best friend, my lover, my soulmate. *I love you Johnny.*

6

Spring came. I was sitting on the back patio with Nigel, the Chow. The only view was of trees, sky, and grass. It was a very peaceful and quiet afternoon. I was reading a book on death and dying and the tears were flowing.

I heard John say very clearly, "For the first time in your life, you have nobody to take care of but yourself. Enjoy it!" The tears dried up and I went about my day with a ray of hope in my heart. Thank you, Johnny.

Toward the end of his stay at the rehabilitation center, it became difficult for Johnny to articulate his thoughts. When a physician or one of the nurses came to the room and addressed me instead of him, I always encouraged them to speak directly to John and to give him a chance to respond, even though his speech had become arduous and slow. This was one more reason for me not to leave his side until he was tucked in for the night. . . .

On the Sunday before he was to be released, friends came to visit. They had come into our lives within the last year, and the connection we had felt was immediate and profound. As soon as they entered the room, my friend suggested that we go to the dining room for coffee. She insisted that it would be good for me and her husband assured me that they would be fine. I remember my throat tightening at the prospect of leaving John, even for a short time. By the time we returned, the room was empty. We found them in a gathering room, John sitting in his wheelchair, the two of them totally absorbed in a discussion on history and World War II. I couldn't believe my eyes . . . for a short moment, a spark of life had returned in John's eyes. One week later, as they walked into our home, she announced that she would spend the night. How unlike her. . . .

That night, John crossed over and after everyone left, I was not alone. It had been perfect timing for a friendship that would be long-lasting. Thank you, dear friends, for the way you touched both our lives.

During the last few days at the rehab, I could barely cope with the overwhelming sadness, as I saw Johnny lying quietly, eyes closed, slowly retreating from our world even as friends visited. One afternoon, a friend came in with a treat she had made especially for him. To our delight, John sat in the bed, took a few small bites, and for that moment, it felt like a surge of life had repossessed his frail body. As grateful as I was, I also knew that a burst of energy often happens as one gets closer to crossing over. Joy and sorrow intermingled as I felt my hopelessness once more.

A day later, as I entered the room, I immediately noticed the peaceful look in John's eyes that seemed to emanate from the depth of his soul. "I just had the most beautiful dream," he said. "I saw this tree. . . . It was the brightest, most radiant tree."

"Describe it to me," I asked.

"There is nothing more I can say," he replied. "It was just so bright. . . . I've never seen anything like this in my life."

At that moment, I knew in my heart that Johnny had begun crossing over to the Other Side. As sad as I felt, I remember thinking how fitting that he would see a tree. . . . Every tree on our land we had planted together, except the one when he had announced, "Come and see what I did!" That was the Maple tree that stands tall and straight today. I was reminded how he loved walking around "the plantation," looking, being, enjoying. I felt much sadness, but so much gratitude for what has been. . . .

For so many years I used the word "comfortable" to describe our relationship. It had taken years of hard work, immense joy, and dreadful pain. But we had gotten "there." We began as good friends. We became so much more. Through the years, he would often say: "I'd do it all over again." I repeated these same words back to him as the illness progressed, and he would say, "I never meant to put you through all this . . ." and he meant every word. Parkinson's took over our lives, but it never changed how we lived. When he left the rehab center to come home with Hospice, we both knew his time was getting shorter. When he said, "Everyone acts as if this is a happy thing. . . . This is about death."

I responded, "It doesn't matter what everyone says, what matters is you and me. We have made the most of every day. Now we'll make the most of every moment."

"I like that," he answered. Friends who visited him that day were Hospice workers and, to our surprise and relief, had come to care for him. What a blessing!

When they laid him in the hospital bed in our living-room, he closed his eyes and never asked for one more thing. I stayed on the couch beside him, wet his dry lips, and told him how much I loved him. Four days later, my best friend and soulmate took his last breath in my arms—and the most excruciating pain pierced my heart and invaded my whole being. The one person I felt totally accepted and loved by had crossed over to the Other Side.

When Johnny took his last breath, I wanted him to take me with him. It had nothing to do with the love in my heart for my family and friends and all that I had to live for. It had to do with the unbearable pain that flooded my whole being. For days, weeks, and then months, that feeling stayed with me as I read about death and dying and the Other Side. There was anticipation through the pain, a yearning to let it all end so I could be with John . . . not with God, but with John.

After months of yearning, wanting, crying, praying, it came to me: Our love had been bestowed upon us by the eternal source of love, God. I had known that all along, but when John died it did not make sense any more. How blessed we had been. How blessed I am now. Thank you Father for so much love. *Thank you, Johnny for loving me so.*

Our very good friends who had grown up with John were coming to visit and stay with me overnight. We had shared many happy moments with them through the years, and I looked forward to their coming. They would stay in our bedroom, so I cleaned and dusted and made everything fresh, including the big armoire with the two open shelves in the sitting room area. On the top shelf were two baskets filled with neatly folded sweaters. The bottom shelf contained two leather albums, a jewelry box, and an oval picture of the two of us resting on an easel. After our friends left, as I entered the bedroom and glanced over to the sitting room, something on the bottom shelf of the armoire caught my eye. I took a closer look only to find my favorite turquoise sweater in a bundle right by our picture. While I was trying to make sense of things I felt John's presence beside me: there he stood, a big grin on his face, and I knew. . . . *Thank you, Johnny, for bringing laughter back into my life one more time.*

7

Today, we were talking about life with you and I said to our daughter: "I still feel very married," as I looked at the rings on my finger. Tonight, in the quiet, I thought of it and repeated the words and the voice I know so well clearly said, "That's because you are."

The macramé wall-hanging in the sunroom reminds me of our life together. You found a yoke with the large, rusted rings still attached at each end. It had been used decades earlier to work oxen and had that rustic weathered look. You hung it on the fence and I taught you knots as we unraveled the brown twine and started weaving a

pattern on the large piece of wood. We often switched sides so the hanging would look somewhat even.

As I look at it today, I see part of you and part of me intermingled on both sides, the parts coming together in the middle and hanging loose at the bottom. The woven pattern of joy, sorrow, growth, communion of souls, and unending love. I will always cherish it!

The coasters depicting scenes of Quebec City have been resting on the coffee table in the sunroom for quite a few years. They are a nice reminder of our many vacations in Quebec. We have used them often and always have put them back in a pile at the end of the coffee table.

As I entered the room as I did every morning, I noticed the coasters upside down on the same spot on the coffee table. I immediately thought of the children who liked to play with them when they visited, but I quickly realized that they had not visited for a few weeks. I always look for an explanation even when I know there isn't one.

Even in the smallest ways, you bring back laughter in my heart and soul. I love knowing that you are near.

For many months, my thoughts were only black. I lived in darkness, and I felt comfortable wearing only black. It was more than the custom I had grown up with. It was something I needed to do out of love, respect, and mourning for Johnny and it reflected the way I felt inside. For many years, I have been swimming at the local YMCA before going to work. One summer morning, I surprised myself. It was not until I got out of the pool and showered that I realized I had brought a bright yellow outfit ornate with a few red flowers. I smiled at myself and thought of Johnny. I felt he was pleased. It was a sunny, warm day . . . all the way into my heart.

8

During the last few months of John's life, our daughter shared with me that every time she glanced at a clock for no special reason, on a wall, on her cell phone, in her car, or anywhere else she happened to be, day or night, the hour would be 1:11 or 11:11. It kept happening. "What do you think it means?" She asked. All that came to mind was the direct line from this Side to the Other, between Heaven and Earth. Shortly after John's passing, no matter where or when, every time I glanced at a clock for no reason, it would say 1:11 or 11:11 and it continues to happen to this day, often when I am questioning where

I am in my life. . . . Coincidence? I don't think so. Something happens inside me every time, like a surge of energy moving through my whole being. Always, I feel a sense of peace and of connectedness with something bigger than what I am living in that moment. It is short-lived but real, and I am grateful.

9

I attended a weekend Twelve Steps retreat as I had many times through the years. This would be the first time I would return home without Johnny waiting for me. I felt very fragile and vulnerable in every way. To my delight, for the first time at such weekends a relaxation exercise was part of the program. I had helped many people with deep relaxation through the years and at a time when I needed it most, someone else would do it for me. I felt gratitude.

It was Saturday afternoon. As my body sunk into the pillows on the floor, allowing my mind to clear and my spirit to be open, I felt the warmth of my tears down my cheeks. I let myself slip into deeper relaxation until, totally unaware of my surroundings, my body became overtaken by warmth, brightness, light, so much light . . . and in the center of the light appeared small beings dressed in white with halos and veils covering their heads, holding hands in a circle, dancing round and round. And in the middle of the circle you stood tall, handsome, wholesome . . . I walked into the circle and you came to me and held me close as the little children danced around us into the light. It was so real, so powerful. Later, lying there on the pillows, the warmth of tears streaming down my cheeks seemed to soak my whole being with love as I bathed in the light with you still at my side.

When Johnny died, I lost all sense of who I was. It was like I had to redefine myself, but I didn't know where to start. Most of all I didn't want to. I liked who I was becoming at his side and the thought of that ending was scary and senseless. I felt lost and without a purpose. I knew I had to live for the people I loved until my journey ended on this side but I didn't know what that meant. I remember asking John so many times to show me how. He has shown me in so many ways and still does. I knew it before, but I have now felt it—love never dies.

My friend, who happens to be a therapist, told me to allow myself "to feel the anger when it comes." I had already told her there was so much pain but no anger; just sadness, an incredible, deep sadness . . . and gratitude for all that had been and all that remained. To this day, there has been no anger, just more gratitude for the love that lives on.

How I longed for you to hold me, to feel the warmth of your arms around me. It was one of those dark days when the pain—the deep, unending pain—held on to me tight from the moment I opened my eyes until I collapsed with exhaustion late that night. And then there was the dream. There were people all around us. "Can you see him?" I kept asking, as you held on to me with strong arms, standing tall and proud. "Yes, we see him, too," they all said. I knew that you were there, alive and well. I touched your arms and felt your warmth. Thank you for coming to me when I needed you so.

10

Going to church and to the grocery store have been two of the most difficult things for me to do. I keep running out of church before the end of the mass. It grabs me—the pain—and it shakes my whole being. I run out and let the tears flow freely into sobs until they dry once more. I keep coming back and I keep running out. On one such morning, a gentleman who had lost his spouse years prior took my arm as I was running out and kindly said, "It will get easier, I know. . . ." How I wanted to believe him, but I didn't think it possible at the time. Someone else suggested I buy two steaks instead of one. I could have bought six steaks and it wouldn't have changed a thing. I am buying for one person, me, and it tears my insides. I go through the motions. I make myself eat but there is no real hunger, no enjoyment of food. The pain, not the food, fills me.

John always found ways to stimulate his mind. He had read a voluminous number of books ever since his high school days and had memorized chapters of some of the classics, numerous poems, and some writings he had found meaningful through the years. He was very conscious of the possible effects of Parkinson's and shortly after being diagnosed had memorized "Casey at the Bat." He would often recite it among friends who marveled at his ability to not only memorize, but to make words come alive as he recited. Shortly before he was to be hospitalized, he had requested a copy of "Casey at the Bat" from the local library to refresh his mind. I brought a copy to the hospital. By then, he had lost interest. Another very sad time. Little by little he was letting go. I knew the day would come when he would also let go of me. More tears, unending tears. . . .

11

Spring was in the air. I hungered for something to bring a ray of hope into my frozen heart and soul. How I missed him. I glanced out the window at the huge lilac bush in full bloom. At one time, it had been a struggling little plant and now it stood tall and strong, almost the size of a small tree. How inspiring! I walked outside with cutters in my hand. The crisp air felt like life hitting me softly in the face. I walked back in the house with a nice bouquet of lilacs, put it in a small vase half filled with water and placed it on a small oak table. The fragrance filled the whole room and for a while it seemed to satisfy the yearning in my soul. A few days later, as the small blooms began to fade, I tried to pick up the vase, to no avail. To my disbelief, no matter how hard I tried, I could not move it. It was like it had become part of the table. There was no trace of water at the base. I was left puzzled and wondering. . . . Days went by, and then weeks. Friends stopped by and made many attempts, but no one could pick up the vase. Meanwhile, I had emptied the vase with a gravy pump and had bought velvet roses to replace the lilacs. No one could explain the immovable vase.

Over a month later, the grandson who remained so connected to John came to visit. "Can I try to move the vase?" he eagerly asked as we walked in.

"You go ahead," I told him.

He tried once and, as expected, nothing moved. "Can I try one more time?" he insisted. He walked to the table, picked up the vase with no effort and grinned from head to toe. "I did it!" he exclaimed. I was dumbfounded. Not even a strong adult male succeeded and now a seven-year-old had picked up the vase with no effort. Not a mark on the table . . . not a smear under the vase . . . and all this time I had been waiting for an explanation. I thought of how Johnny had insisted on giving me red roses on our last Christmas even though Jessica had offered to shop for him. I smiled to myself. They were not real, but the red velvet roses had brought warmth, color, and life all the way into my heart. *Thank you, Johnny for bringing me roses, still. Je t'aime.*

The first summer without Johnny, I sat alone on the swing, often losing track of time, waiting for him to come and sit beside me, to hold his hand, to eat cheese and crackers and salami, to be silent together.... The weeds grew, the sun didn't shine, the soft rain didn't comfort me, and the trees stood still. I just sat there and waited... until one morning when I found him sitting there in his faded plum shorts, wearing no top, and tennis shoes without socks. I sat beside him and felt his arm around my shoulders. We sat quietly. I remember not wanting the moment to end. Then I was alone again.

Every morning, that first summer, I felt like I could not get through one more day, not with that intense, tearing, cutting pain shredding my whole inside. Not with my aching heart that wanted to burst out of my chest. Not with that heavy weight that kept me from taking the next breath. Not with the abyss always waiting for me only a few feet away. Not with the deep longing that could not be satisfied. Not with that dreaded time late each night when I would crawl into bed and you wouldn't be there. Not, not, not. . . Yet, the first summer came and went and I survived.

For many years after John's passing, I put off going to bed. "I waited all day for this . . ." he used to say as we cuddled up in bed. We never fell asleep without our bodies being molded into each other the way we had since the beginning. As the illness progressed and it became too much pressure on his frail body, words like, "Let me put my arm around you" or, "Give me your hand," were just as meaningful. We loved any way we could. After Johnny crossed over, only exhaustion, late at night, sent me to an empty bed.

It has been almost two years. I still have the pillow with the blue flannel case, the one he took his last breath on, and the navy pajama top he last wore, beside me in our bed. I often find myself smelling them, looking for a remnant of his scent . . . it fills my whole being. To this day, I still wrap myself in his blue plaid robe and feel his warmth all over me. *Johnny how I miss you.*

A few weeks ago, I filled the trunk of my car with John's clothes and took them to my angel from the Rehab, known simply as Sister Sam. Until that day, every time I had opened his closet all I could do was look, touch, smell, and as tears started to flow, close the closet and walk away with that heavy feeling in my heart. Two years passed. One day I asked Johnny to help me. Tears rolled down my cheeks, but I got started. I couldn't give away all of what had been him, but eventually bags and bags filled the trunk. His razor is still on the vanity and his slippers at his bedside. His favorite jacket is hanging on the hook. I might get to it someday. Not now. Somehow it brings me comfort.

12

It was a stormy night. Thunder and lightning. Then it came, a deafening peal of thunder that resonated through the whole house. I trembled in my chair, stunned and frightened. I instinctively turned my head and there you were, standing tall by the dining room table looking at me with a look that said, "I'm watching over you." It lasted an instant but at that very moment I knew I was safe. Thank you, Johnny.

The grandchild who misses you so and remains so connected to you has felt your presence, sometimes at ball games or just riding in the car with his parents. "Grandpapa is here with us," he would say. Often in the morning he would recount how you had twisted his nose at bedtime, the way you used to when he was little. It seems all so natural to him. It brings us both comfort.

You never cared much for "popular" songs, by your own admission. But that one song you said was the exception. I listened to the words with you and I was touched to the core of my being. Once in a great while I hear it play and it still touches me in the same way. The song "After The Lovin'" by Engelbert Humperdinck is a beautiful reminder of the way we loved.

13

The outdoors continues to be a source of solace and healing. As often as I am able, I begin my day outside on the back patio, looking at trees, grass, and sky. This is where I so often find you, this is where I read, eat, write, cry and cry some more, but always with a sense of peace that "passes all understanding. . . ." How grateful I am for the beauty you have brought into my life. I love you, Johnny.

It seemed such a short time, thirty-two years together. After you crossed over, surrounding myself with pictures of you, of us, was painful and comforting all at once. I could only look at recent pictures; I could not bring myself to look at anything else. It felt like I could hang on to you that way. It took months and months before I realized the physical changes that had taken place as your illness progressed. Then, one day, the letter came from MCO. There would be a memorial for the people who had donated their bodies for the benefit of science. The medical students requested pictures to honor the deceased who had contributed to their education.

Painstakingly, I began going through albums of pictures: pictures of family gatherings, pictures of summer vacations at the chalet, and pictures of so many wonderful trips with close friends. As much as I dreaded going back in time, it was an incredible healing journey to piece our life together from the beginning through albums and albums of pictures. This was our life. This was who we were, who I was, and who I still am. I felt connected to you, to what we were as a couple and a family and to what we had become. After a while, thirty-two years did not seem like such a short time anymore. Reconnecting with the past filled gaps that had been lost in grief. Life had been full. There had been challenging times, growing times, sad times, and fun times. Somehow, life started to make some sense again. The memorial was a wonderful tribute to you and to all who had contributed to life and to mankind. It brought tears and sorrow and so much healing. Once more I felt grateful for all of life as I was reminded how I loved who I was becoming beside you.

14

This would be my first time away without Johnny, a vacation to Florida with our daughter and her family. I had had many experiences of his presence in and around our home and leaving the familiar was threatening to me. I did not feel or believe that I had the strength to go away without him. They told me I was going, that it would do me good. I remember telling John: "I am going, but you have to come with me." We had spent the day at Disney and we were all exhausted. It was late at night. Shortly after climbing in bed, I felt a strong presence, Johnny's presence beside me. I remember having to move in bed to make room for him. He put his arm around my waist and held me tight, the way we used to fall asleep. I felt safe and went to sleep. *Thank you for loving me all the way to Florida.*

After Johnny died, when nothing made sense, I found meaning in the littlest things . . . the flowered umbrella, hat, and pouch he had given me for my birthday; "Aloysius," the small bear with a zipper he had bought for me for Christmas; the knitted blue hat and gloves that I seldom had worn and the burgundy wool shirt with the gray felt leaves that I had admired in a magazine. How much they mean to me now.

"Do you have another of Grandpapa's pajamas?" asked the grandchild who, like me, was searching for you in any way he could. He had just found out that I slept with your pajama top. I gave him your blue flannel top. "When I am cold, I wrap myself in Grandpapa's pajamas and he warms me up all over," he still reports even after a few years have passed.

For months and months, especially on the darker, most painful, emotionally draining days when my heart aches for him with no relief in sight, I have been aware of the abyss patiently waiting for me. At times, I would see myself walking to the edge, looking down at the infinite darkness, tempted to let go. . . . At other times, I would be just standing there for what seemed eternity, reluctant to walk away. But today was different . . . today I saw myself walking away from the abyss with a deep knowing that I would not return. Today my step is a little bit lighter. Today my gratitude overflows.

15

Every night, at dinner time, I continued to set the table for two, for you and me, the way it had been for over thirty years. In the last few months of your life it had become difficult for you to sit at the table, so I would always make sure that your chair was in the right position as if you were to come to the table and sit down with me. Time after time I sat down and waited, feeling sad and barely able to eat; food did not taste the same without you. I had lost so much weight already that my clothes seemed to float around me. Family, friends and co-workers were concerned. But it didn't matter. Nothing seemed to matter.

After months and months, one night I surprised myself by placing one setting only, in Johnny's spot. I sat down and looked through the picture window. To my amazement, it felt like I was looking at the view through his eyes . . . the huge Sycamore, the evergreens we had planted alongside the road, and the swing. Somehow, I felt relieved. That night, for the first time, I would eat alone and I would be okay.

I would often think of how I enjoyed cooking for you, for us. I would remember earlier times after you retired and began to cook. At first I would leave all the instructions and ingredients on the counter, sometimes even a list of pans needed to prepare the meal, before I left for work. Then gradually it happened . . . you began preparing your own meals, then you went grocery shopping, then you brought home exquisite recipes you copied at the library. Often, I would walk in to the sight and smell of a wonderful meal on the table. Other times I would be greeted by the smell of fresh baked bread even before I entered the house. I cherished those times then and they mean even more now. Today, I sit in your chair, eating a good dinner while glancing at the peaceful view of trees and sky and I feel warm all over.

After you died, I knew I would never hear the words "Je t'aime" again. I thought with certainty that the most meaningful words I ever heard you say had died with you. How wrong I was. Shortly after you passed on, the grandchild who often felt your presence and slept with your pajamas began following his "I love you" with an immediate "Je t'aime" as he ended a phone conversation. I am not sure how this came about since I had not shared my thoughts with anyone, but it warms my heart every time I hear the words still to this day.

16

A few months before you left, we had purchased a love-seat with La-Z-Boy features so we could be comfortable together and better able to sleep at night, but early on it became too much for you to get in and out. The lift-chair sat beside it and I would often squeeze in with you, breathing with you and holding on to you. For the last four days of your life, a hospital bed stood in its place. This is a sacred place for me. The place where you took your last breath. The place where heaven and earth met.

After you passed on, I made the only decision I knew you would feel comfortable with: your lift-chair would be passed on to other families living with Parkinson's disease. The love-seat that was meant for both of us was moved into its place. That night, as I walked into the room, I heard your voice, perfectly clear, asking: "Where will I sit?" "Here beside me," I replied as I motioned to the love-seat. Your presence has been felt there so many times since, often greeted with incredible sadness and tears, but in the last few months mostly with joy in my heart for the love that lives on.

It was fall, his favorite time of the year, almost two years after Johnny had passed. The night before, through an intense and painful emotional and spiritual struggle I had released him once again so he could be all that he was meant to be on the Other Side. Once again, the tears were flowing and I finally fell asleep totally drained in every way. Early the next morning I let the dog out into the pen and nonchalantly looked up at the sky. To my amazement, there were contrails wide and fluffy all over the blue sky. A plane was flying right in the middle of them adding to the enchantment. I stood there mesmerized by the beauty and thought of Johnny, who always noticed contrails. He had worked on airplanes during World War II and seemed fascinated by contrails. As I kept looking up at the sky, I couldn't believe my eyes . . . golden birds were flying south, as gold and as bright as the rising sun shining on them from the east. It was a sight to behold! The wonder of it all still lives in my heart and in my mind's eye. Thank you, Father. *Thank you, Johnny.*

17

Thanksgiving has come and gone. It was happy and comforting to be with our daughter and her family. Today I am finishing decorating the house for Christmas. Not much—lights in the windows, three small trees, the crèche, and garlands on the mantle. Everything reminds me of you; everything makes me ache for you. Halfway through it, it all came crashing down inside me. The pain, the tears, more tears . . . life felt so complete with you. It feels like a waiting game . . . waiting for death to deliver me from my prison of despair so I can soar with you and feel whole and free. But I know someplace inside me I really want to live . . . for the people I love, and yes, for myself. Help me live, Johnny. . . .

Later that same day I walked with our Chow. And there you were walking beside me, firm, steady steps, wearing your red knitted hat, olive green jacket with suede collar, and yes, gray sweats . . . and tennis shoes. I've said it before; I'll take you any way you come . . . I came in feeling lighter inside, with a small ray of hope welling up in my heart. I knew I would be okay. Thank you, Johnny, for helping me go on.

The following day I let Nigel out to his pen late at night. As always, I looked up at the sky. It appeared deep and dark with fluffy clouds that could have been pure white snow. It was like the earth extended into the heavens. The full moon glowed with orange and pink rays wrapped all around it. Such beauty! I was in awe and felt immense joy in the pit of my stomach.

"How does it look from where you are?" I asked Johnny. Immediately I felt a strong presence, the presence of the Divine. "You have such good taste," I whispered to myself.

The following Sunday morning on my way to church I said these words to John: "I want you to be free and soar like an eagle." Walking from the parking lot, I looked up at the blue sky and saw a seagull fly over the steeple of the church and head directly toward the sun until it disappeared into the brightness. Love filled my whole being.

18

The first New Year's Eve without Johnny, I remember retreating into the bathroom to be alone with him as midnight was approaching and our friends who had celebrated so many New Year's Eves with us were getting ready to welcome the New Year. I wiped down the tears and came back to the room. Everyone welcomed me back with hugs and kisses. They knew . . . they missed him, too. A few hours later, as each couple said good bye, I asked every one of our male friends if the gray knitted hat on the back of the couch belonged to them. They all said no. After everyone had left, I immediately checked the coat closet where John's jackets were still hanging, his knitted hats and gloves on the shelf. His gray knitted hat he always wore with his Icelandic black and gray jacket was missing.

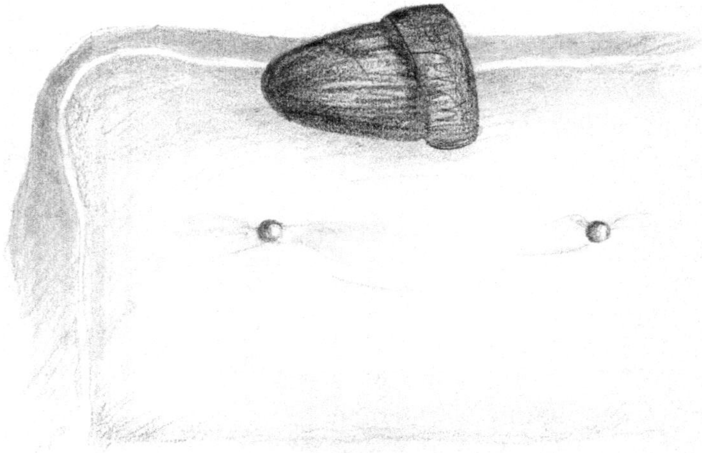

They had said you would be with me. How right they were. How I love knowing you are near.

After many attempts at releasing Johnny as the seasons came and went, always through extreme sadness and unending tears, I was given a special gift—the awareness and understanding that Johnny wasn't mine to release. With this revelation came the freedom to enjoy his presence without questions or a lingering sense of guilt. *Thank you, Lord, for a beautiful gift of love.*

I was watching a show on PBS and I thought of how interesting it would be to Johnny, who loved history. As I continued to watch, something very intense took place that I cannot explain to this day. I came back to full awareness with my left hand clinging to my shirt at the neck. I knew I had just experienced watching the show through John's eyes . . . like he had been part of me. I felt totally connected to him with my whole being. After a few minutes, I got up and walked directly to the dining room, where a picture of the two of us on our last New Year's Eve together stood on the hutch. In this photo, I am sitting on John's lap and his left hand is clinging to his shirt at the neck, the exact same way I had just experienced. I was stunned by the depth of what I had just lived. . . . *Je t'aime.*

Early on in our relationship I realized that something more profound than I had ever experienced in the past was developing between Johnny and me. There seemed to be a freedom of being and living that was totally unfamiliar to me. For many months, it was only that, a friendship where acceptance of where each other had been and where we were now seemed to exist. Over time, as the friendship grew into something more, the connectedness which was there initially deepened and expanded inside and outside ourselves. The bond that united us became stronger and more meaningful as we shared our most intimate thoughts and emotions openly with each other. It took heartaches, joy, commitment, and determination, but through it all we both recognized that what we shared was more than either one of us had thought possible.

What I did not realize until John's death is the impact

we had had as a couple . . . people had noticed. They had seen the closeness and had felt the energy and the passion in daily living that emanated from both of us. It was all there in the sympathy cards . . . the personal notes not only about Johnny, but about us and what we meant as a couple to friends and even to acquaintances and people that we had known only from a distance. They had noticed "us." I had no idea. I cried, I laughed, I mourned, and I rejoiced. I knew that what we had was real. I hadn't realized how many people knew it, too. They were grateful for him, for us. How grateful I am to them! They loved him; they loved us.

A few days before the New Year, I was pondering the word "lost," which I had used to tell a friend how I felt. As I began to identify times where I had felt lost, I was left with the sensation of the deep, familiar ache inside me, an ache that had become part of me. And suddenly, there it was ... in my mind's eye I could see the ache in the form of a dark tube that appeared hollow at first glance but, as I looked closer, was closed in at both ends. The black, metallic, somewhat threatening tube emerged from the left side of my "center" while the rest of my being looked bright and peaceful. I sensed some movement within the dark tube and I had some expectancy that something would be revealed to me and bring me understanding. But for the moment, the tube was just there and I had to accept it as part of me, which was a little frightening.

That night, as I kneeled by the bed, something happened way deep inside . . . the black tube broke open with pieces of the black metal spilling into my center. Then from the open tube a burst of light came to life. I waited for the light to illuminate my center, now engulfed in semi-darkness, hidden by a dark cloud. But it did not happen. I felt exhausted, climbed into bed and fell asleep. As I awoke the next morning, something wonderful happened. In the left side of my center where the black tube had first appeared, I saw brightness in the shape of a cone from which emanated beams of light and the brightest stars I have ever seen, all flowing into my center, illuminating, radiating, and warming my entire being. The ache I had felt and seen had been transformed into a joy-filled and lasting renewal of mind, body, and spirit. I was not lost anymore. I could go on. *Thank you, Father. Thank you, Johnny.*

19

It is New Year's Day, my second New Year without John. Two years ago, we were sitting at the Bistro in the sunroom quietly enjoying Christmas music, the warmth of a blazing fire, and snacks from New Year's Eve. I can still feel the closeness and the peacefulness of that moment even though we both knew there might not be another New Year's Eve together. The same friends who have been with us to celebrate the New Year for so many years were here again last night. "We want to be there with you," they had said. "We know John will be there for you." Tears streamed down my cheeks as midnight

struck, the ball came down in New York Times Square, and everyone kissed to welcome the New Year.

I am grateful for the legacy of love and friendship John has left me. But this New Year's morning, the ache in my heart for John was almost unbearable. I needed to feel his presence, to know he was still with me. I prayed and cried and told him how much I needed him. Sitting in the living-room in the exact place where John had taken his last breath, I felt alone and desperate. And then it happened. Suddenly I felt John's presence in the room, but it was more than his presence . . . it was an incredible feeling of love that filled the whole room, so much love that the room could not hold it all . . . it felt like the walls were pulsating, pushed out to make room for this moving force of energy.

My whole being was filled with love. I knew in all my senses that I had been heard. God was listening and he had allowed his love and John's love to fill me. I felt so blessed and so loved.

This is New Year's Day, and I am grateful to God for having you in my life, Johnny.

20

A very dear friend who had shared many humorous moments with John would often say: "When I grow up I want to be just like John. . . ."

A few years after John's passing, he felt an inner prompting of the Spirit, "to go to the Huron Library." He followed that prompting and went to the Huron Library, which he had never visited before. He walked in, looked around, went up the stairs to the adult section, took a turn and ended up in the spiritual section. Noticing a book buried between two other books, curiosity led him to uncover the hidden book. Its title: *Love is*

Stronger than Death, by Cynthia Bourgeault.

"I read it and I knew it was meant for you," he told me. I started reading and could not put the book down. Someone else had lived a love that remained alive and vibrant beyond this world. For the first time, I didn't feel alone in all the extraordinary experiences I was living since John's passing. I knew they were real but I now knew that someone else had lived something powerful and wonderful. How grateful I am for you my dear friend, for the book and for Cynthia Bourgeault. What a blessing!

Warmer days have returned . . . without you. I have been feeling lost again these past few days, yearning for you, wandering aimlessly, unable to focus. This weekend I went to visit our daughter for a special celebration. As we drove to the event, I felt your presence in the car. You put your arms around me. My eyes watered. I was grateful. That night I had a dream. I was in a room with some of our friends when you walked in. We had both been away and I thought you might be upset that I had not called. Instead, I heard you say: "That was some trip—I ended up in a ditch." Then you looked at me and added with your often "twisted" sense of humor: "You'll have to plan better." You sat on the couch and I put my arms around your neck, felt your beard, and kissed you on the cheek. "I missed you," you whispered. "I missed you, too," I replied. "Come here and I'll show you." You had that look I knew so well, the look that says: "I love all of you. . . . You didn't seem to care about the people around us. "I'll start by removing my gloves," I said almost shyly. I woke up in the middle of the night filled with so much love. Thank you for loving me so.

A friend shared with me that a short while after her husband died she began finding pennies everywhere, even in the most unlikely places. "Pennies from heaven," she called them. I had never heard of pennies from heaven and even though Johnny had passed on more than a year earlier, I had never found one penny. I let the thought go quickly. There were so many painful, often excruciating moments in my daily life. Pennies, from heaven or not, did not matter much. Months later, pennies began showing up . . . everywhere . . . at the airport, in bathrooms, the shower at the Y, by the car door in parking lots, on the floor inside the car, in the yard, in restaurants' entryways, driveways, gatherings, etc. etc. etc. "Pennies from heaven!" They are real!

21

I had a dream. I was lying in bed dozing off. You came in, lifted the covers and said: "Move over . . . you thought I was gone, but I am here . . ." I felt your body against mine. I kissed your cheek. It was soft and firm. Your hair was short and dark. I looked at your face. "It is really you, you really are here?" I asked. I held on to you as I drifted to sleep. I love you Johnny.

I had just finished reading a statement of Christ, found in Luke 5:34-36, "Jesus said to them, no one tears a piece from a new garment and sews it on an old garment; otherwise the new will be torn, and the piece from the new will not match the old.'" A few days earlier it had become clear to me, as I reached yet another level of understanding, that I needed to love John for who he was now, a spiritual being enlightened and unfolded in the love of the Supreme Being, God. Anything less would be saying: "You are not enough." At that moment, I had a greater awareness that I did not need to touch him to feel him with me.

As I sat quietly, letting Jesus' words permeate my mind and heart, I had a vision. The "new" was just plain lightness, like a blank slate the color of a pale sun. Then above it came the "old," a ray of brownish gray that seemed to be shooting out from the past; it had distinct lines on either side as it got wider and wider over the light slate. As the dark ray got further out, the bottom line seemed to dissolve, letting the darkness spill out onto the light slate and they became part of each other, the old and the new as one. How comforting to realize that I did not have to keep looking back, that the old and the new were here in this moment. . . .

I could continue with you always alive in my heart and soul, the old a part of the new, whatever that may be. Thank you, Jesus. Thank you, Johnny.

It is early in the New Year. I visited Sister Sam today. She was the angel who took me in her arms the morning I heard the words: "Last stages of Parkinson's." I guess I knew all along, but hearing the words was devastating. John was going to die. Facing the fact that there was no hope, I felt broken and defeated. Sr. Sam, whom I had never met before, just seemed to appear as I stood outside the room sobbing.

She put her arms around my shoulders and softly whispered: "I thought you might need me." A wonderful friendship developed from that very moment.

Today, we sat quietly for a while, watching the ducks and geese flapping their wings playfully and gliding on the pond, creating white caps in the dark water surrounded by snow covered grounds . . . a sight to behold! After a while, Sr. Sam took out a bag filled with pieces of bread and called out: "Goose, goose. . . ." Hurriedly they came out of the water and up the hill. One large goose ate right out of Sr. Sam's hand and the rest of them feasted on the "manna" scattered on the ground. A beautiful scene! Later, Sr. Sam led me to the chapel where stood a rocking chair. There she told me a beautiful story about God, our loved ones, and the rocking chair. Then she left the room. I sat there in the peace and quiet, tears streaming softly down my face, as a new understanding came to light . . . it is not the pain that gets deeper over time; it is the connectedness to John's spirit. Thank you, God. Thank you, Sr. Sam. Later that day as I walked into the sunroom, my eyes lingered on the rocking chair. . . . I felt uplifted, with reverence and joy in my heart.

22

I have not cried today. My eyes have watered a few times, but I have not cried. I did not cry yesterday either, even though I remember wiping my eyes a few times. It will be two years next month that Johnny died. We just had another snowstorm, one of many in the last few weeks. Today I was out in the snow, shoveling, feeding birds, and walking the dog. Everything was white everywhere and it was cold and windy—freezing cold, but sort of cleansing for the soul.

Nigel and I started up the road as you and I often did. Then you appeared, walking beside me with a steady, firm step, wearing your black snowsuit with burgundy scarf and hat, brown gloves, and tan laced boots. Your beard was frosted from your warm breath. We walked together for a while. My heart felt warm as I told you how much I loved you, that I will always love you. I thanked you for walking with me and "your" dog. I thought of how you had insisted that he was mine although you had named him and trained him. You wanted him to be mine so he would protect me when the day came. . . . Today as I walked with you and Nigel, the knowing that this is our life together now somehow nestled way deep inside my being and I really knew it was going to be okay. You with me the way you are and me with you the way I am, our spirits never apart from one another. I couldn't touch you, but I could see you and I could feel your presence. My world, our world is well. Later, I stood by the window, pensive, watching birds. Four bright red cardinals decorated the white snow. I thought of you, how you loved watching birds. Suddenly, I felt you beside me, your arm around my waist. We watched the birds flying back and forth from the evergreen to the bird feeder, scattering seeds all over the white snow, for what seemed an eternity. . . . Alone again, tears started to flow, but there was joy entangled with the sadness. Through it all, I wouldn't change a thing. Je t'aime.

23

Today is your birthday. I got up this morning, hugged your pillow, and wished you a Happy Birthday. I wondered what it's like on the other side on your special day. In my mind's eye, I could see you in the middle of a crowd of people born on the same day, having a wonderful celebration. Are you celebrating? Then I wondered what your special day would be like for me. I had an agenda, things I couldn't fulfill yesterday. But for now, listening to Josh Groban and Placido Domingo, I let the tears come.

After a while I walked into the dining room, pulled up the blinds, and looked out at the white blanket covering the ground. Right away I noticed the bird feeder on the ground by the pole where it hung. I thought it was strange since it is made of clay and heavy enough not to be dislodged by even high winds through the winter. As I walked to the front door, I noticed something on the floor. I picked up a small, bright red flower that belonged in the crystal vase on a table quite a distance from where I found it. I smiled to myself as I wondered how it had gotten there. I tried to dismiss it as nothing spectacular, just like the card I received for your birthday, now standing by your picture on the wicker trunk, when I knew very well it had been laying there since the day it had arrived; just like the sock in the paper basket in our bathroom; just like . . . just like . . . so many little things that would make me smile . . . I walked outside by the bird feeder and quickly realized that in no way could the ring on which it was suspended have traveled up the rounded pole carrying the bird feeder until it fell to the ground, still attached to the pole by the

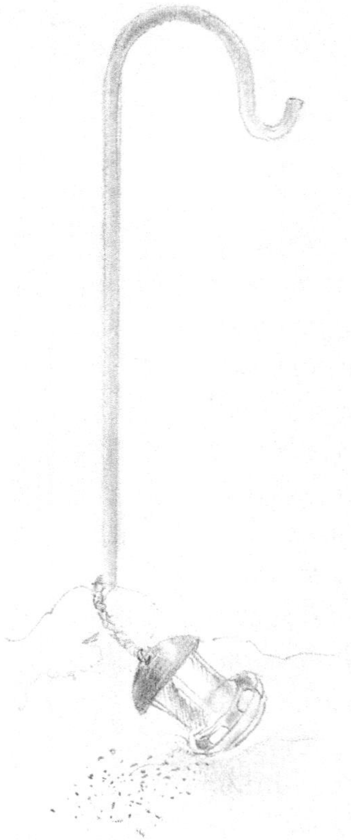

small rope from which it hung. In no way could I explain how this had happened. Even a wild animal could not have pushed it up that high. I began to laugh . . . a sock didn't do it, the card standing didn't do it, the red flower on the floor didn't do it . . . the bird feeder on the ground still hooked onto the pole did it!

Happy Birthday, Johnny! I love you with all my heart. I had a plan today, a sad one, but you and God had a different one. . . . I took our Chow for a walk. The air was cold and crisp, the snow was falling softly and it felt good. You walked with me part of the way, in your dark snowsuit and red hat and brown gloves. I felt joy! Later, friends came over and we planned a trip to Toronto and went out for a bite to eat. They wanted to celebrate your birthday with me. They miss you, too. At the restaurant, we sat at a table where you and I sat so many times through the years. They talked about you. I talked about you. The tears came . . . even the waitress had tears in her eyes. I got home and settled down on the loveseat to watch a movie. I felt your presence and made room for you beside me. It was a special movie and a special night, having you at my side. Thank you for spending your birthday with me.

This is Saturday morning, one week after your birthday and a few days from March second when my world crumbled around you. It will be two years. The heaviness that for so many months had been like a constant companion that I learned to tolerate and then grew accustomed to has returned this past week. It is heavy and dark, way deep inside, and I feel like I am waiting for it to burst out of me.

On your birthday, there were soft tears but nothing heavy. Just sadness.

This morning I walked into the sunroom the way I do most mornings. As I opened the French doors I stopped . . . the draft stopper snowman that had been sitting against the couch for months was now lying on his belly, legs extended, about one foot from the couch. I stared a few seconds and thought: *Could it be me? Could I have tripped over it the night before and have not noticed?* Then I remembered walking out of the room the night before and turning around as something caught my eye; it was a dead leaf close to the snowman and I walked away thinking I would sweep the room tomorrow. It was then that I realized that something had happened and it wasn't me. I burst out laughing and said out loud: *"I am so glad you're here in the house with me. I do not want to doubt any more. Thank you for being here for me." Maybe this week will be happy and joyful . . . I just said joyful . . . just the thought of it . . . that is BIG!*

24

It is a beautiful spring day. Walking up our small country road with Nigel this morning, I noticed the red leash wrapped around his collar and stopped. As I bent down to fix it, my eyes were immediately fixated on a small object standing right at my feet in the middle of the road . . . I could not believe my eyes . . . a penny standing on its side, perfectly erected, right at my feet! All anyone knows in my very small neighborhood is that my husband died. We wave and say hello. I picked up the penny and looked at it with disbelief as tears flooded my eyes. A penny standing up on its side right at my feet in the middle of my small country road . . . it is still in my coat pocket and every time I touch it I am reminded how much I am loved!

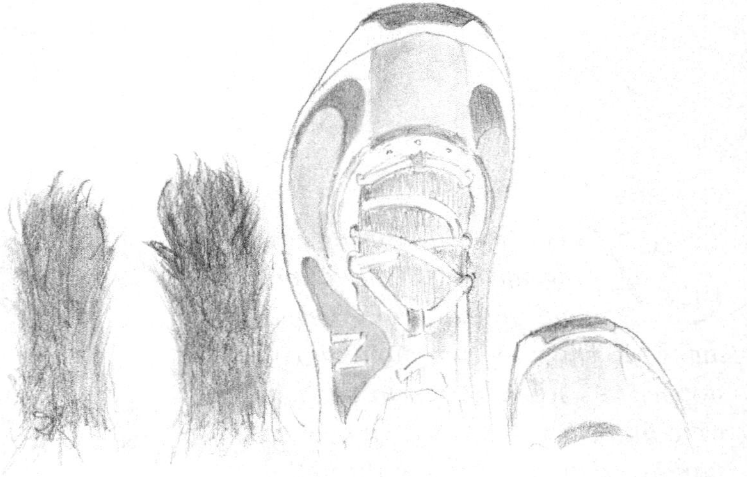

For the longest time the pain went so deep inside me, it felt like it shredded every ounce of my being. The heaviness in my chest was sometimes unbearable. I often struggled to breathe. But after a while, through the intense pain came a glimpse of joy and it became all entangled . . . the pain and the joy as one. Tears still flowed, but at times there was more joy and even laughter. One day, the joy stood alone, at first for a moment, then for a day. In these moments, I felt the joy of being alive . . . just breathing and being . . . Almost unthinkable but real! I am grateful for all of it.

Looking back on the first summer still brings a shiver through my entire body. I would sit on the swing and tears would flow. It often felt like my heart was about to burst out of my chest, like there was no more room to hold all the pain. The beauty around me made it all the more painful. It was something we had lived and breathed together for over thirty years. That summer I bought a few baskets of flowers. The flowers were beautiful but there was no harmony in the colors that kind of clashed and I remember thinking that they reflected the way I felt inside, just a patch of mixed, entangled, painful emotions. This summer I bought flowers and the colors are vibrant tones of red interspersed with patches of white and they reflect the love and peace that are growing in my heart and taking more space every day. I am grateful.

25

You had wanted a truck for quite a while but had decided to wait until your car died out on you. It did, on the fourteenth of February in the snowstorm—the accident that would exacerbate the symptoms of Parkinson's and propel our lives in a spiraling decline. You would not be driving anymore but you certainly could ride in your new truck. You did. Today I decided that the time had come to trade in the truck that had become too much for me to handle with groceries, etc. The gentleman pulled up your name on his computer and asked if I knew you. Immediately tears started flowing and I couldn't say a word. The man apologized profusely, without having any idea until I let him know that I had not expected to burst into tears at a car dealership but that I had everywhere else since your passing and I was going to be okay. I needed more time. I left and went home.

Late one night, sitting quietly and reviewing in my mind some of the events of the last few months I felt a strong presence beside me, a loving, comforting presence. . . . "Father, why did you choose me to live this. . . ." I asked. Soft tears turned into sobs. "Tell me it's not my imagination . . . please tell me that it's real . . . please show me . . . I don't want to live a lie. . . ." I cried out through my sobs. I was in so much pain, I felt like my chest was going to burst open. Then it was calm. I was calm. Only the soothing sounds of crickets outside the bedroom window could be heard. "You have given me enough signs . . . why am I questioning you," I muttered, not knowing if this was for God or for Johnny.

Exhausted, I crawled in bed, pulled the covers over me, and drifted into a deep sleep. The next morning, walking out of the bedroom I glanced at the picture of the two of us on John's dresser. Taken many years ago at an army reunion, he has his arm around me and we are both smiling. *"What did I do?" I heard the voice I know so well say. "I'm not upset with you," I replied. "I'm upset with myself for doubting you." I glanced back and the words just poured out of me: "I'm not afraid to embark, Johnny, it's just that at times I'm afraid it's not as real as I think it is. I will go wherever it takes us. . . ."* Later that night I thought of how feeling so connected to John brought me the deepest pain and the greatest joy. I wouldn't change a thing.

26

It has been three long years and I continue to miss you, to want you. . . . But lately I have noticed an uneasiness about me. Maybe it comes from my dreams, where you are present but always in the distance where I can't reach you. Are you pulling away from me or is it my way to let you go? Why now? I wondered. Then it came to me—when a close friend and physician who had spent hours and hours with you in the last months of your illness said that from his experience it took two years to get through the grieving process, in my own psyche I gave myself three years before I could "move on," whatever that *meant. Well, three years had come. . . .*

One day, soon after, I remember asking you, "Help me do this," as I removed the pillow case you took your last breath on and put your pillow back, next to mine where it had been for three years, with a fresh cover on it. It felt like a breath of fresh air!

I often hear friends talking almost casually about their deceased spouse and I find myself asking myself: *How long will it take you?* with the certainty that that day will never come. How can it? My best friend and soulmate has passed on. It takes all the energy I can muster to continue living. Joy has become a welcomed companion at brief intervals but I am still at the stage where the pain gets unbearable at times and tears flow at the most unexpected places. This is what I am living, and again, I wouldn't change a thing.

I was driving home after a long day at work. I glanced at John's picture in a small oval frame in the car. I had placed it there as soon as I got the new car so it would be our car. I was thinking how after more than thirty years being together every day, I was coming home . . . alone. *Before I could finish my thought, I heard the voice say: "No you're not!" I smiled and said, "You're right . . . I'm sorry."*

27

Three years have passed since you crossed over to the Other Side. Today, a very warm summer day, I sat on the swing after a long walk with our dog. Instantly, I felt the now familiar ache rising inside me. I so needed to feel your presence. . . .

As my mind drifted to the many times we had spent sitting closely, quietly, looking at the sky, the trees, I felt your arm around my shoulders. In that moment, only love filled my soul. I sat quietly, grateful for sharing another amazing moment with you.

Tonight, as I stood on the front patio, a beautiful Monarch flew by, getting closer and closer to me, first in my hair, then on my shoulder, then playfully fluttering around me. It flew away and soon came back, landing on my chest, slowly creeping up my tank top until it reached the ring on the chain around my neck, your wedding ring, and it stopped. Tears were flowing down my cheeks as I kept telling the Monarch how beautiful it was. I put my finger close to it and it slowly wrapped itself around it. I kept talking to it, crying and laughing. Then slowly, this beautiful butterfly with a slightly torn right wing made its way into my hand, touching it repeatedly with its long, slender "tentacles." I could feel the light touch in the palm of my hand. After a few minutes of "pawing," which felt like the gentle brush of a feather, the butterfly flew away and landed in a bush a few feet distant. I walked toward the bush and in the blink of an eye the beautiful butterfly disappeared.

As I slowly walked back to the patio I felt fluttering on my right arm. The same beautiful butterfly with the torn wing had returned. I reached with the index finger of my left hand and, as it had before, it carefully wrapped itself around it. It slowly moved toward my right hand and, as if understanding my thoughts, the tiny creature slowly made its way back into the palm of my hand, feeling its way with its long "tentacles," touching my skin over and over with an incredible softness. Emotions burst out of me! I cried, laughed, talked to it, repeating over and over: "You are so beautiful! Thank you."

The butterfly seemed very content to be nestled in my hand. From time to time I brought it closer to my face as if wanting to make sure this was not a dream. I was really living this incredible moment . . . with a butterfly. It was exhilarating! As I stood there for what seemed an eternity, I felt a deep sense of joy and gratitude for sharing life with one of God's most beautiful creations. It was about noon and the sun was scorching. I heard our dog barking from his pen on the other side of the house. "I have to get Nigel in," I found myself telling the butterfly. "Will you come in the house with me?" The butterfly continued "pawing" in my palm. "We're going in," I said and opened the front door. I walked into the house with my precious friend, through the living room, dining room, kitchen, through the back door, mudroom, garage, and opened the last door to the dog's pen.

We were now outdoors again, but my precious friend showed no sign of wanting to flee. I walked back into the house with the dog and my precious friend, walked to the bedroom, talking to it, asking it if it had seen this room before, walked back through the house, sat in Johnny's chair at the dining room table, looked out the window, called my new friend "John" and said: "This is what you so enjoyed looking at." After a while I squatted down by the dog to show him my little friend still nestled in my hand.

Our dog weighs over eighty pounds. There we were, the three of us. I am sitting on the floor with a butterfly in the palm of my hand and our big black dog is sniffing it as close as he can get his nose, almost touching it. "How do you like our new friend?" I asked Nigel.

As I attempted to get up, my foot slipped and my beautiful friend flew up into the French doors. I opened the doors into the sunroom and the butterfly flew in, up into the skylights, into the windows, the plants, and back up into the light. I opened the door to the back yard, but my friend showed no interest in flying away. It was just gallivanting all over the room until it finally was done playing. It landed on the door frame.

I extended my finger and the beautiful creature wrapped itself around it one more time. We walked outside together the way we had come in. I watched the beautiful butterfly fly away. "I will never forget you," I said. The feelings welling up inside me were beyond words. Even as I write, it's like there isn't enough room inside me to hold it all. *Thank you, thank you, thank you!*

28

The Holidays have come and gone. My third Holidays without you. The last few days have been filled with heaviness in my chest, cloudiness in my mind, and a profound and insatiable yearning in my soul. These were just unending dark days and nights where I forced myself to go through the motions. But today, something is different. Today, there is a tingling in my soul and the vibrations are resonating in every part of my being! For the first time in three long years I feel like the scattered pieces of my existence are coming together.

Maybe through the darkness I have come to accept your death all the way into my bones *and in every cell of my being. Today, it feels like the hurt and the pain are no longer an ache inside me but have become part of my inner self. Today, for the first time in a long, long time I feel connected in body, mind, and spirit. Today, I feel a deeper connection with you; a deeper acceptance of you as a spiritual being. Today, in this moment, I feel whole. Thank you!*

Sitting by the window in your favorite spot where I so often find myself, my eyes fixated on the peaceful scene of trees and sky, I watched, in a trance-like state, as my hurt and my pain drifted away from my being, enfolded in a gray cloud that floated away on an unending dark road.

As I watched the cloud vanish in the darkness, I saw myself walking toward the light, a warm, inviting, embracing light . . . I came to, staring at the beautiful scene of trees and sky with a deep knowing that something beautiful and profound had touched my soul. Today, I feel lighter way deep inside. Today, I feel joy in loving you.

29

It was a warm, breezy summer day. Nigel the Chow and I were taking our daily walk up our narrow country road when a beautiful Caligo butterfly flew by and landed on my shoulder. Its deep colors of charcoal gray and the brightest blue were so mesmerizing, I could not take my eyes off it. I was totally consumed by such beauty. We continued walking, slowly, the three of us.

As Nigel and I turned around at the top of the hill, the beautiful butterfly flew away and before I could wave good bye, there you stood beside me, plum shorts, striped polo shirt, gray tennis shoes, and no socks. We started walking down the hill, the three of us . . . I felt warm all over, overwhelmed with gratitude.

Today, grief is taking me back to the struggles of the past, our past, remembering and feeling the pain of self-doubt, questioning my motives, your motives, my reactions, your reactions, and wondering how or when I would feel peaceful again. Looking back on those challenging times, the only thing I would change is I would be kinder to myself. Even though they were painful to get through, today

they seem minimal compared to the closeness and the blessings they brought into our life together. And with each challenging time came the knowing that peace always returns once the "letting go" lets go.

I woke up from a nightmare with deep sadness filling my whole being.

"I need something from you to feel joy again," I muttered half way into the morning, not knowing whether I was addressing God or Johnny. Early that afternoon, sitting by the window with the two grandchildren and their parents, "Look, a hummingbird . . . no, it's a yellow finch!" our daughter exclaimed.

At that instant, the yellow finch flew from the hummingbird feeder right to the window, fluttering its wings back and forth in an amazing dance as we watched with fixated eyes, holding our breath not to chase it away. After what seemed a very long time the yellow finch flew away only to come back momentarily and repeat its little dance all over again as if to dissipate any disbelief. Writing about it still fills my soul with joy and wonder all over again. *Thank you, God. Thank you, Johnny.*

30

It wasn't perfect. You had your ways and I had mine. We both had our past hurts to deal with and although it was good from the beginning, it sometimes seemed easier to pay the price of not sharing feelings openly and freely, building walls of anger, resentment, and poor self-image, and when all else failed, blaming our behavior on each other or remaining silent for a day or a week. Yes, there was a lot of adjustment, and painful times were interspersed through the good times. I remember "pouring my heart out" to you and promising myself—never again—as nothing was said in return. I never could keep that promise. I still remember the day when, after one of those intense, emotional times, the words came out of your mouth like a breath of fresh air: "I don't know how to talk about feelings . . . I wasn't raised that way." Little by little our walls crumbled as we both became willing to make ourselves more vulnerable and eventually open ourselves up to life and to each other. Life is about change. Our life together transformed itself in ways I could not have imagined or dreamed of. Little by little, acceptance replaced judgmental attitudes and unrealistic expectations.

Our relationship became "comfortable" with spontaneity and excitement woven all through, and over time, permeating every aspect of our life together. We began as friends thirty-two years prior. Over the years, we became best friends and soulmates. We knew this because it was spoken. The separation of body, mind, and spirit seemed to vanish. Touching and feeling became one, and thoughts met and often intertwined, and "two will become one" became a reality. Life became fuller and every moment mattered. It was all so worth it!

31

It was a hot summer night. The water felt warm and soothing on my tired feet, sinking in the sand while the sounds of the waves resonated all around me. I could not move, mesmerized by the gracefulness and intensity of the ocean. It looked as dark as ink in the distance. I stood, immobilized, contemplating the magnitude and power of your works, Lord, my feet sinking deeper into the sand as the foam from the forceful waves dissolved at my feet.

I had never experienced the warmth of the ocean on a hot summer night. The constant movement of the waves, the vastness of the dark body of water touching the sky in the distance, the stillness within my soul—the immensity of it all was engulfing my whole being. The sun was setting bright and pink under a large cloud to my right, but in this intense moment, my eyes stayed locked on the ocean, all my senses partaking in the beauty and magnitude of your works . . . the sound, the smell, the movement, the waves splashing all the way up my knees. I could almost taste the saltiness sticking on my hands as I reached down to feel the wetness.

This was a moment of reckoning, a moment of truth. I felt so small and so alone and so lost, with a deep yearning in my soul for you, my God. "Take me," I muttered, tears gently flowing down my cheeks. At that very moment, the

Presence in white garment stood in front of me, bigger than life, arms extended, looking at me, and for a moment I saw the face, your face . . . this I know, even though to this day I have no recollection of it. The voice sounded deep, coming from on high, "I AM with you." Tears streamed down my face as I heard my own words: "Take me with you." This wasn't a dream. The Presence was real, calming, and overwhelming all at once. The sun had set. As I stood there, eyes fixated, I thought of my friends waiting for me. I had to go.

"Stay with me," I cried softly.

Before I turned away I heard you say: "I am going with you."

As I slowly started walking away, the Supreme Being, now in a human size, walked beside me. A part of me had been yearning for Johnny. "Where is John?" I asked, more with my eyes than my words. And there was Johnny, to my left, wearing only his faded plum shorts, barefoot in the sand, his hair blowing in the warm breeze, walking with us. I stopped to pick up two sea shells that stood out in the sand, one very light, the other one a little larger and darker. When I stood up, I was alone.

One of my friends walked toward me and put a dark gray shell in my hand. "This one is from me," she simply said. I wrapped my fingers around the three shells. *Thank you, Father, for such a special gift of love, friendship, and beauty!* I didn't feel alone any more. My friends and I had a nice meal in a cozy little restaurant and went back to the hotel. I could not sleep that night, as the immensity of it all hovered over my whole being. My soul could not hold it all. I got up and began writing. I never told my friends. At that moment, it was too much to process. All I could do was to let the words pour out upon the paper until I was done.

Remembering, it still feels that way. How blessed!

Quite a while later I saw the production, "Jesus Christ Superstar." It was a tremendous and moving performance and I thoroughly enjoyed it. I do remember thinking that this wasn't the voice I had so clearly heard months earlier. . . . "I AM" still resonates within my soul, though I cannot adequately put the words into sounds. I can only cherish the still vivid encounter, the words vibrating inside my whole being, encompassing all my senses, my heart overflowing with love. Again, I am filled with gratitude.

I have been praying to love you as the spiritual being who touches my life every day and to not keep longing for what used to be. Today I feel it in my heart. Yes, Johnny, today you are enough just the way you are.

For so long I was not able to find joy in this newfound freedom. I went to work and went through the motion of living, but my heart was not in it. Then one day it happened . . . life felt complete again. It was a very ordinary day. I was sitting on a chair in the dog's pen. Nigel was lying down at my feet with a big smile (he does smile) and Evangeline, the orange cat, was in my lap. I heard myself say: "Life is so complete."

My own words resonated way deep in my soul. I smiled, looked up and said, "Thank You." For the first time since Johnny died, life was complete again. Whoa!

That same day, a few hours later, I felt this ache for you in the pit of my stomach. I missed you with my whole being. Tears wet my cheeks, but not for very long. Gratitude rescued me . . . gratitude for all the years . . . the inner turmoil . . . the inner peace . . . the unending love . . . gratitude for it all! A friend had asked me a few days earlier if I ever wished I could have one more hour or one more day with you. "No," I replied. Everything had been lived, spoken, felt, and done. All I could ever wish for is another lifetime with you. I am grateful for you, and for me and you.

32

I am back there again . . . back in a dark, cloudy, almost threatening space inside myself. For no apparent reason, I find myself caught in the web of inner turmoil of years past. It is at times almost as unbearable as the pain of losing you. I am caught in the times of struggle, inner struggle filled with questions and self-doubt encompassing all aspects of life—mine, yours, ours—times when the space between us seemed so large and deep that I wondered if we could touch again, times when I felt, way deep inside my being, that I wasn't enough, times when I knew I was loved, but did not feel it in my soul.

But as the darkness begins to lift, of its own accord, I find myself thinking of the times when one of us or both of us started reaching out again, touching, talking, feeling, sharing, knowing that the place we had gotten inside ourselves was not meant to hurt each other and that we still retained the ability to say, "I'm sorry." At those times, I felt an inner brightness, like a warming sun, embracing us in an ever deeper, more meaningful way of relating to each other. Always I felt grateful for the "waiting." Always the acceptance of one another grew easier and deeper until, finally, our souls touched in a way we didn't know existed.

I mourn the closeness and I mourn the more challenging times that, a little at a time, brought out our vulnerability and opened our hearts and souls to let each other in all the way. This had been part of what we had lived together and I needed to feel it again—the pain, the joy, and the freedom of letting it go one more time. This is part of the moving on, made of the beginning and everything in between. It is the end of summer. The butterflies are now leaving. I suspect they will be back next year. The cardinals are now touching my life the same way they touched our lives.

Our dog still lies beside me on the back patio and seems to enjoy the stillness as much as I do. I let the new cat come inside the house and I know you approve. . . . The sky is still the most beautiful blue and the trees, our trees, continue to bring a soft breeze that whispers of God and of you. I have let you go and yet more than ever you are with me every day, in everything I do, thoughts I have, things I say, and everywhere I look. Most of all I feel you in my heart, your soul touching my soul . . . forever grateful.

I was sitting by the window, reading *Healing after Loss*, by Martha Whitmore Hickman. It talked about being at death's door with our loved one. I glanced at the stillness of the landscape outside the window . . . and then there was no awareness of my surroundings as the vision occupied every fiber of my being. A huge door made of wood with a gold, shining handle, stood high in front of me. The thought came, as if from outside myself: *You are on the Other Side . . . and the large wooden door is closed.*

Momentarily I noticed a wide opening on either side of the huge door that allowed a flow from the Other Side to my side and back again. The movement between the two sides suddenly gave way to a large archway where the wooden door had stood, leaving wide open the way to the Other Side. On each side of the archway, light veils swayed back and forth, moved by a gentle breeze that was almost palpable. The scene was bright and cheerful, even inviting. At that very moment came the understanding that the Other Side was really a breath away. The vision faded as gently as it had appeared. Looking out the window, the words softly came out: "*Thank you for the gift! You are only a breath away. . . .*"

A few days later, after reading about having realistic memories of our loved ones, I was sitting quietly, pondering the meaning of some of the words, letting my thoughts take me wherever they might. Thoughts ceased to exist as a huge screen with large squares made of wire appeared before me. The next instant, what seemed like hundreds of white butterflies coming from the left passed through the screen, and flew up to the heavens in the brightest light. And there we stood, you and me, your arms around me. . . . Another gift! I love all of you, the way you were and the way you are. . . .

33

"I am so full of life!" The words spilled out of me so loud and clear that I surprised myself. "Oh, my God. . . . Thank you!" I exclaimed. I had been walking with Nigel the Chow, watching the "big grin" on his face as he looked at me playfully. "You are smiling aren't you!" I stood in the middle of the road and looked up at the most amazing blue sky with bright pink and violet clouds. The beauty all around me was electrifying and I felt the excitement permeating every cell of my being. I felt alive, joyful, and whole all at once as my soul captured the beauty of the canvas painted by the Ultimate Artist.

It was then that I felt so much light spill out of my being. At that moment, I was reminded of the dark funnel I had seen within myself several years earlier while on a soul-searching journey and how, months later, while driving to work on a country road, that funnel had opened wide, spilling so much light out of me that I had to stop the car to take it all in. It was like being one with all that existed! I felt like dancing in the middle of the road. That same light had flooded my whole being again, bright as the sun and vibrant with anticipation of a newfound freedom.

That night I was remembering—the closeness, the warmth of your embrace, the cuddling up at night, our bodies molded into one as we drifted to sleep. How I missed all of you. . . .

Then, there was the dream. There were young men all around the room, aspiring young men gathered around the young, slim, dark-haired woman. They seemed to be waiting, while she didn't pay much attention. An older gentleman, tall, handsome, gray hair, and beard, walked into the room. He reached for her and she found herself dancing in his arms while he gently led her into a spacious room that spoke of medieval times with dark ornate stone walls with only a large, soft white bed. Then, in the distance, at the end of a ray of light, two lovers laid, their bodies entangled on the white sheet, the wetness between them keeping them as one a little longer through the night.

I awoke with tears running down my face. "You were there. You were there," I kept repeating to myself. It was a dream, only a dream. But for a while, the memories were alive. I felt your touch, your warmth, your breath, your hair, all of you. You were there. Thank you, Johnny.

34

I had gone to a retreat, a "Desert Day" retreat where you spend quiet time searching your soul and listening to God.

Sitting on a bench under a tree, looking at the wonders of creation, and feeling very small in the midst of it all, I found myself drifting back to the last three years of your illness: how I got through the fear of losing you, the feeling that I couldn't go on, the unending sleepless nights, the worrisome days away at work, the fear that it would never end and the fear that it would, the anxiety of unanswered calls, the physical, mental, emotional, and spiritual exhaustion and, through it all, the heartfelt gratitude for having you in my life. I thought of the poem "Footprints in the Sand" and how well that described my own life.

While still pondering the miracle of life and death, I had a vision of my whole self, shrinking to almost nothingness, disappearing in a funnel of darkness and then, after a few moments, noticing a small speck of brightness in my shrunken self slowly growing and suddenly exploding into a huge ray of light where I came out whole, vibrant, and full of life. Thank you, Father, for carrying me in my darkest moments and for reviving my spirit!

I've often heard it said that grief never ends, it only transforms itself. Someone who had lost her husband shared that, "It only gets deeper." I believe that all of this is true.

It will be four years since you left me and yet you are still with me every day, in my thoughts, in my life, in the things that happen without logical explanations, in my dreams. But mostly you are with me in the happy memories—things that you often said, humor that made people laugh, poems you recited, the way you grinned with amusement, all these things that are so you. I remember the many occasions when you would bring up a subject you and I had discussed, only to make me repeat a word that I had pronounced with a strong French accent, for the sole purpose of our friends' amusement and laughter.

As many times as I had confronted you about it, your answer had always remained the same and with the same grin on your face, "Everyone can say it right . . . no one says it like you." To this very day, I refuse to pronounce certain words that our friends would like to hear. . . . The most incredible thing is that now I can experience you in every way with joy in my heart! What I thought impossible is becoming reality. For the most part, the endless anguish and sorrow that tugged at my heart every time I felt your presence or relived a memory have now been replaced with peace and happiness. How often I prayed to feel joy again and today, loving you brings more joy than tears. For any of the ways you continue to touch my life I am grateful.

I was pulling weeds by the hammock on a warm sunny day when I noticed a butterfly dancing around my feet. It landed on my bare toes and seemed to be playing around. After a while it flew away and I walked back to the patio and sat down. The butterfly quickly reappeared, danced around my face, and landed in my hand. It was a small, unassuming, brown and taupe butterfly. "Will you spread your wings for me?" I asked softly.

To my amazement, the butterfly immediately spread its wings and remained still long enough for me to explore every aspect of this tiny being. With its long "elephant proboscis," it repeatedly "pawed" at my hand, to secure its next step as it moved slowly from one hand to the other. The subdued colors of dark brown all around the wings, the taupe body and the small white circles at the lower part of the wings with white brush strokes at the top gave it an elegant allure as it continued to move gracefully in my hands. Unlike the experience of the previous summer, this butterfly's wings

were shaped perfectly. In its humble form, it felt like the most beautiful thing I had ever seen. It didn't seem to have any intention to leave, so after a long while I decided to take it inside the house.

I got up from the chair, opened the sliding door and walked into the house, the butterfly still gently "padding" my hand, like a cat making its bed. I took it into every room, most of them recently remodeled due to a water problem, and began addressing the butterfly as "Johnny" as I showed him all the new improvements. The butterfly went from one hand to the other, gently kneading my skin with the long, delicate "elephant trunk" that seemed to guide its every move. I finally walked back into the sunroom, opened the sliding door, and watched as the butterfly left my hand and flew up toward the sky. *Thank you, God. Thank you, Johnny, for a wonderful visit.*

The following day, walking from the mailbox, I felt a gentle touch on my feet. The same butterfly was again dancing around my feet before landing on my shoulder and then in my hand. I slowly walked back toward the house with the butterfly gently tapping on my fingers. I sat down on the back patio and just watched as the butterfly moved slowly from one hand to the other as it had done the day before, feeling the delicate touch on my skin and the love welling up in my heart. The sun was shining bright and hot so I decided to walk to the swing where "we" could be in the shade. The butterfly spread its wings and I raised my hand close to my nose so I could see every aspect of this small, so great a creature, in all its beauty. It was the same one with the same markings as yesterday. The dark and light browns, the taupe body, and the white brush strokes on the top of the wings, six on the left and seven on the right and the white circles on the bottom of the wings, four on the left and five on the right.

All my senses were awakened to the magnitude of what I was experiencing. I was having a relationship with one of God's most amazing creatures, a small, unassuming butterfly "who" was choosing to spend time with me. We were totally connected in some inexplicable way, and we both felt it. What a miracle of life! After quite a long time, as the sun was going down, I told the butterfly that I had to mow the grass before dark. Soon after, the butterfly flew away. I walked away from the swing with an exuberant feeling in my soul. I had been touched to the core of my being by one of the most gentle, unassuming creatures on this earth. The image of this butterfly is imprinted in my mind and it brings tears to my eyes as I relive every detail of that incredible encounter. I am grateful!

35

I am letting go. . . . Today I had the courage to gather some of the special clothes I was still hanging on to—the clothes you wore in our last photos together; the clothes that touched your body and kept you warm as life was being drained out of you; the clothes that had lost your scent as the months turned into years—I folded them neatly and put them in a bag for Sister Sam. She always finds people in need. I am also letting go of some of the pictures—the framed picture of the memorial where you donated your body to science; pictures of us taken during our last New Year celebration, our eyes filled with sadness;

other pictures reminding me of your illness—they are now safely tucked in the small wicker trunk filled with memories of your life and accomplishments. I am letting go . . . but I still feel the love, alive and vibrant, within and all around me. Thank you, Johnny.

I have been having nightmares where you are present but not available to me. There are always other people who seem to be interacting with you. How I wish you would come to me and just be with me for a while. But you do not seem to be aware of me. When I wake up, a sadness lingers in my soul until I consciously let go of another bad dream. After a few weeks of recurrent sad dreams, I began to wonder about the message . . . what was it I needed to see?

One morning it came to me: forgiveness. I slowly began to say the Lord's prayer, believing in my heart that there wasn't much I could consciously or unconsciously be holding on to, surely not about Johnny. We had weathered many crises, growth-provoking circumstances, and painful events. Through it all, we had come to know an understanding and an acceptance of each other that allowed us to touch each other's soul and to know a kind of closeness neither one of us knew was possible. We had spoken these words. That's how we both knew. By the time Johnny passed on, the thought that everything that needed to be said had been said, all the way to the very end, was very comforting.

What was left to do? Grief, at some point, encompassed all the experiences we had shared through more than thirty years. . . . The good and the bad, the best and the worst, the emotional upheavals and the incredible moments of pure ecstasy, the joy and the pain that brought on the kind of closeness and connectedness that is seldom spoken of.

Finally, the light came on in my mind and I understood. I needed to forgive him, Johnny. He needed my forgiveness and I needed his. I forgave and asked that he forgive me. The nightmares stopped. He was free and so was I. Forgiveness: one of the final steps in letting go, in being free.

36

In the book, *The Year of Magical Thinking*, Joan Didion uses a phrase from the movie "Robin and Marian" by Richard Lester—"I love you more than one more day."[1] As I read the words, I knew immediately . . . Johnny had refused the feeding tube to be inserted into his stomach, being fully aware that it would shorten his days on earth. As painful a decision as it was for both of us, he would not rescind it. Looking back at what I had become after three years of caring for him night and day while keeping up a seemingly normal work schedule—the weight loss, the lack of appetite, the inability to sleep, the exhaustion, the worry of leaving him alone, the knowing that there was no going back. . . . In every way, I felt like a shell of what I used to be. So many times he would say: "I never meant to put you through this," and so many times I would reply that he would do the same for me.

Then there was the rehab center—preparing his favorite foods and watching him painstakingly swallow two or three bites, the anxiety of leaving him at night, the sadness of knowing the end might be near, the tears flowing all the way home, often driving in inclement weather and icy roads. Through it all came the most rewarding moments of two souls touching each other in the most intimate dance of intense feelings and emotions about living and dying . . . there was the closeness, the spoken words about the fear of letting go, the holding on to each other lying on the hospital bed, the depth of the intimacy as a priest who had known John for decades gave us communion (breaking the host in half), the love and support of Sister Sam, family and friends. I would do it all over again. I have no regrets.

After a month, Johnny was coming home . . . to die. He had refused the feeding tube. He was reluctant to come home. "You can't do this alone anymore," he said. I reassured him there would be some assistance. On the day he was coming home, the nurses were fussing around him. "This is about death . . ." he said sadly. "We lived every day to the fullest, now we will live every moment to the fullest," I replied. "I like that . . ." he said. He was home four days. They laid him down in the hospital bed in the living room. He closed his eyes and never asked for anything more as I often stroked his face, wet his lips, and told him how much

I loved him. Through the following days and nights, family and friends gathered around him, talked to him and let him know how much they would miss him. On the last night, he whispered so, so softly. . . . "Let me go . . ." and I finally mustered enough courage to say the words . . . and a few hours later he was gone. I knew why he had refused the feeding tube. And I knew why he laid down quietly to die. "I love you more than one more day."

Earlier that evening, our daughter had climbed in bed with him before returning home to her family and had told him how she wanted to be here to hold his hand when the time came. She had also told him that if he and God had other plans she would understand. She was safely home when he passed on.

[1] Joan Didion, The Year of Magical Thinking (New York: Knopf, 2005), 68.

37

I have let go. . . . Today I am becoming aware of things I have left behind. As I read my daily meditations, it suddenly occurred to me that I had not been reading *Healing after Loss*, by Martha Whitmore Hickman, a book with daily meditations given to me by a friend, a book I had read religiously every morning ever since I had received it. I have no recollection of when I stopped reading it; I just know it happened.

I am also aware that I have let go of "needing" to feel your presence, to relive specific moments. I have not kissed your pillow every single night, looking for your scent. I now wear the gold chain with a cross and your wedding ring only on occasions, as a beautiful piece of jewelry, but always as a symbol of our love. I have also let go of a "tradition" as our friends referred to our New Year's Eve gatherings for the last twenty years, or more. As much as I have appreciated their love and support, greeting the New Year became a painful experience without you. It was time to make a change and these past Holidays I did! Though living fully in the moment, no matter how intense the pain, he has turned my sorrow into joy . . . I still miss you every day and I feel the love, always.

38

It has been four years. The past few weeks I found myself in tears every day, often sobbing uncontrollably, with an overwhelming sadness clouding every instant of my waking hours. It felt like grief, in its deepest and most intense state, had repossessed my soul and crushed my joy into small pieces of unrecognizable matter. But even though once again life stood at a standstill, just when I thought I had found a new sense of freedom and "joie de vivre," I found, inside the all-encompassing sadness, a deep knowing that something big was stirring inside my soul. . . .

As the days went by, a new understanding emerged and I became aware that I was grieving "letting go" of my grief. I shared some of my thoughts, feelings, and experiences with our priest, a compassionate and gentle soul who shared some of his experiences with the death of loved ones. Soon after, I felt lightness in my heart as the overwhelming sadness lifted and joy once again filled my soul. I am grateful for the sadness and the tears that led to another letting go. This is a big one . . . it will take time . . . but I know I'm on my way. I let grief take me wherever I needed to go; I will stay on the path of letting go and see where it takes me, with you in my heart, always. . . .

39

All through the years I always spoke the words "I Love You" in my native language and early in our marriage John repeated them back to me. On occasions, he would send me a bouquet of wild flowers. One bouquet came with a card where he had simply inscribed the words "Sha Teim." This is how the words "Je t'aime" had sounded to him. How precious! It brought so much joy and laughter in my soul. I tucked the card away and never referred to the spelling.

It is a beautiful sunny morning. Today, I am ready to move on, to leave the sorrow behind, to embrace fully the joy welling up in my heart and soul. Today, I am ready to continue this incredible journey, loving the moment, loving life, loving you.

Sha Teim.

40

The pain of losing you was so intense and so encompassing that for the longest time I needed every room to contain it. I looked at our home as a sanctuary, a sort of shrine where the years we spent together were depicted on pictures, pillows, and the sacred place where Heaven and Earth met on March 2, at 9:45 p.m. It was to remain a shrine in your honor, a place where time stood still, a place where every emotion experienced during the past thirty years seemed to fill every room, a constant reminder of two hearts once beating as one.

It was all there—for you, when your

spirit needed the familiar so you knew where to reach out; for me, as the assurance that our love would stay alive. I do not know when, exactly, the transformation happened. I just know it did!

Today, there are still pictures of you, of us. There are still lingering emotions. But today, our home is not a tribute to your death; rather it has become an oasis where life is celebrated daily, yours, mine, ours.

There are still times of incredible sadness, times of mourning you, but mostly there is joy, life, sunshine, laughter, and this home can hold it all! A tribute to you, to unending love, to fullness of life. What a gift!

Today, the only sanctuary left is the old wooden swing where we so often sat and where I shed so many tears after you left. It is a sanctuary to honor your love of birds. Colorful bird houses and bird feeders adorn the old swing where birds of all colors and species dance gracefully in and out of their little domain, spreading empty seed shells all around as they playfully fly between feeders and evergreens. Only the wind sways the swing softly back and forth as it whispers of you. I love watching the birds and I know you are watching with me. . . .

41

Yesterday I went walking in the quarry with a visiting nephew, his son, and Nigel the Chow. As we walked down the sloping path, you passed me at my right, jogging with a firm step, in your faded plum shorts, turquoise and plum striped polo shirt with a white collar, and gray tennis shoes. You appeared bigger than life, strong and full of vigor. I followed you down the path, my eyes fixated, unable to utter a sound. What would I say anyway . . . my nephew had no awareness of our encounter. Further down the path, I watched you stop, turn around, and stand with wide open arms and then *you folded your arms around me, tenderly embracing me . . . a heartwarming, silent, joyful moment. . . .*

This is a beautiful morning—the sun is shining, the wind is blowing, the leaves in the trees are alive with sound and the birds are loud and joyous. The bright red cardinal has returned, as it has for several days, making its way around the large forsythia bush, the natural "curtain" shading the large window, tapping on the window with his beak as to say, "Good morning, I'm watching over you."

You loved cardinals and they always bring comforting thoughts of you.

This morning, the room is alive with whispers of you. I love you!

I was sitting by the window reading my daily meditations. I closed my eyes to experience the moment more fully. At that very instant, I entered a space deep within myself and saw the funnel, radiant with light, emanate from the center of my being. It felt like the brightness shot out of the funnel, becoming wider and wider. In the ray of light appeared beings that I had first encountered at the retreat weekend during the relaxation exercise, a few months after Johnny's passing.

Small in stature, with white halos around their heads and wearing white garments, they formed a circle, dancing round and round . . . while you stood in the center, tall and handsome. You stretched out your hand and pulled me into the circle, your arms around me, dancing and twirling. . . . You never cared much for dancing, but in this moment your step was light and you moved gallantly around with complete ease and confidence. You took my breath away!

I do not know if it lasted a few seconds or minutes, but as suddenly as it had appeared, the brightness receded into the funnel in the center of my being. Just as suddenly, the funnel inside me opened again and I felt myself being shot out into the light with such force that it reminded me of a space ship. In that instant, I could see the whole earth from up above and the next instant my feet were brushing the surface of the ocean and then barely touching the top of mountains, bouncing around in the open space. It was exhilarating! In a flash, as fast as I was blown out into the light, the funnel once again disappeared into the center of my being and I was brought back to reality. During this extraordinary experience, even though I remember feeling tears streaming down my cheeks, there was no other awareness of my physical self or my surroundings. As I sat by the window, tears still flowing, words were pouring out into the stillness of the room: "It's all inside me. . . . It's all inside me . . . ." I felt so much joy that my being couldn't hold it all. *I felt connected to the universe, to my Heavenly Father and to you, Johnny. I am so grateful. Thank you, thank you, thank you!*

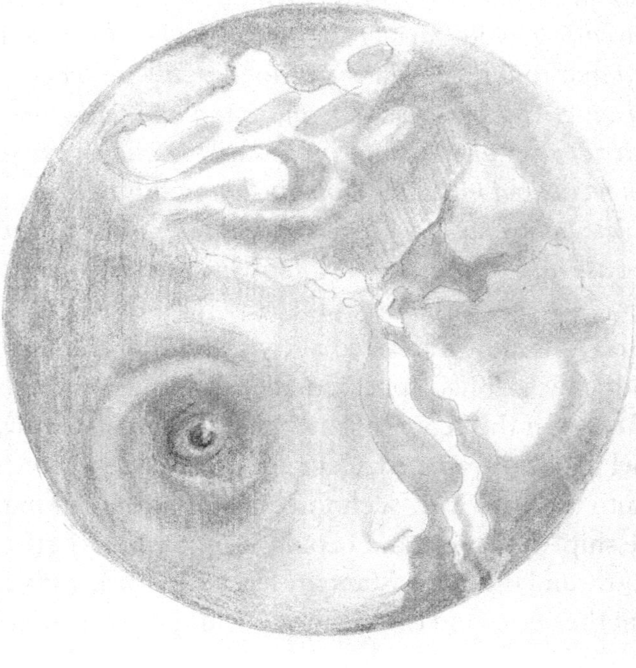

Moments later, as I attempted to put my encounter into words, images vividly appearing in my mind's eye, my thoughts suddenly were interrupted by this incredible vision of my whole being extending itself beyond any physical limitation, effacing any boundaries with the outer world. I felt surrounded by an infinite, rippling circle of love that reflected like the ripples on a calm lake where a stone has been thrown into the water. As time stood still, the calmness and peacefulness were almost palpable. In what seemed only an instant, I was back, pen in hand, thoughts of what had just happened flooding my mind faster than I could put them on paper. I remember praying to feel joy again, but never could I have imagined or dreamed of such intense joy surrounding and filling my whole being. As so many times before, gratitude filled my soul.

As the years passed and I continued to experience you in so many ways, a time came when a deep knowing awakened in the depth of my soul, the knowing that you had reached your destination on the Other Side. You had stayed for as long as I needed you, no matter how often I attempted to set you free through tears and sorrow. . . . Today, we are both free . . . and yet our love lives on. . . .

In the joy and the fullness of life there are still times when my heart aches for you . . . like right now. . . .

42

Yesterday was Valentine's Day. In a dream, among family and friends, you came to me, all dressed up, standing strong and tall. You put your arms around me and I can still feel the warmth of your lips pressed against mine. . . . I love you, Johnny.

Last week was Johnny's birthday and tomorrow is the anniversary of his passing. Even though the Lord has turned my grief into joy, there are still times when an incredible sadness fills my soul, the way it has for the past few weeks. Today is Sunday and I was away with family most of the day. I came home to be greeted by Nigel, our Chow, and Evangeline, the Orange Tabby.

Moments later, I poured myself a glass of water and as I reached into the freezer for ice cubes I was instantly immobilized by the sight of a penny on the ledge inside the door. Laughter filled my soul and the whole room. I knew without a doubt that I could not explain this. There has never been any money on top of or around the refrigerator . . . and there was no one around but me.

Thank you, Johnny! The sadness has lifted and the joy has returned. Tomorrow, with joy and gratitude, I will place red roses where your ashes are buried, knowing that our love lives on. Pennies from heaven?

43

Six years have passed. I am more conscious of time now. Last night I opened a box of photos I had sent John's sisters through the years. They had been returned to me when the last one joined the family on the Other Side. I have been simplifying a bit more with everything and I thought it was time to discard all these pictures, which were doubles anyway. While doing so, I was listening to music of days gone by . . . beautiful love songs.

Suddenly, there came over me this incredible, powerful longing for you. Tears flooded my cheeks as I became aware that tearing apart all these pictures of you, of us, of the family, felt like I was throwing our whole life away. The tears felt warm on my cheeks, almost comforting. Then it was over. The tears dried up on my face and life went on . . . no more unending tears. And the journey continues. . . . Sha teim.

Later, much later, on a cold winter day, I reached for my tan suede boots at the back of the closet. I slipped the left boot on and as I tried to slip the right one on my foot, something blocked my toes. To my disbelief, the whole bottom of the boot was filled with dog food . . . the third time

around, disbelief quickly metamorphosed into sheer amazement! No one else had been around and the boots had been neatly placed on the braided rug in the back of the closet since the previous spring. . . . I burst into laughter, so loud that it shook my whole being.

It had been a challenging time and I had thought you were not there to help me through it. . . . How wrong I was!

44

It has been seven years. Yesterday was one of the hottest days of the summer. It has been hot, humid, and rainy for days and the weeds have taken over much of the "plantation." This morning I began weeding around the Snow Fountains Cherry we had planted in Johnny's remembrance. I weeded and weeded until sweat burned my eyes. It felt good to see the rich black dirt around the tree and beyond the field stones that define the area not only of the tree, but of John's ashes buried under the round, heavy stone. I liked how it all looked and I knew that Johnny did, too.

The next morning, I walked into the sunroom, looked through the sliding doors, and felt pleased at what I saw. I sat down and began my daily readings. As I glanced again at the tree, I noticed something. . . . Could it be??? The stone covering Johnny's ashes was raised . . . again! I rushed outside, tears filling my eyes as I looked at the stone standing against the tree. Only a small indentation remained in the dirt where it had laid, like a hand had displaced a little dirt on top of the ashes. Nothing else was disturbed on the ground where the stone had laid for so long that it had sunk in even with the ground. I stood still, attempting to take it all in.

After what seemed an eternity, I knelt and slowly put the stone back where it had laid and a moment later, it looked like nothing ever had happened. I knew in my heart that what my eyes had just witnessed was something big, beyond anything that the mind could understand or explain but, nevertheless, it had happened. The image of the stone standing against the tree and the undisturbed ground around where it laid is imprinted in my heart forever.

Words of John Denver's song, "Perhaps Love," often resonate in my heart, a reminder that love survives and thrives . . . into eternity.

I am fully aware that most of what I have lived with Johnny following his death cannot be explained with the rational mind. Nevertheless, I know with certainty that I could not, of my own will, have created these experiences. This I have lived. This is how my healing came, and I am grateful for all of it.

Sha teim.

This folder with the stack of notes is what became the book Je T'aime. I do not remember exactly when I started going through the pieces of paper depicting the experiences of the first few years of my grieving journey. As I began reading, each piece of paper brought back the raw, intense feelings and emotions that were embedded in every fiber of my being. The only reference to time was "It has been two years . . . or three years. . . ." This was my way to piece together the fragments of my life after Johnny crossed over. During this process, it never occurred to me that there might be a book someday. This was too personal to share with anyone. Only a few years later, after the messages in my spiritual readings talked about sharing experiences, did I slowly open myself to the idea of sharing my journey with others who are grieving a loved one. With the encouragement and support of family, friends, and people put in my path at just the right time, the book took form. This is a very humbling experience and I feel privileged to have shared my journey with you.

Epilogue

It has been over a decade since Johnny crossed over to the Other Side. Sometimes it feels like a lifetime has passed, and at other times like he just took his last breath in my arms. . . . As grief continues to metamorphose inside my whole being, it has become a welcome part of my heart and soul as it still manifests itself in ways that are now so familiar, but without the intensity and the frequency of the first few years. Looking back on my healing journey, I am filled with gratitude for the love that has endured through life's many challenges and that has remained alive and strong through death and beyond.

For many years after I "reentered" the world of the living, there was a gnawing in my soul, letting me know that I had to share my journey. As often as I tried to silence it, the message became clearer and stronger, now coming from people in my life who wanted to know, from outside sources who knew little about it but believed that I had a message worth sharing, and from books and spiritual readings that unmistakably tugged at my heart, letting me know that my journey was worth sharing.

I have always said that I would rather pull weeds than sit at my computer. As much truth as there is to this, it became my excuse to not share my journey, until I finally came to terms with my reluctance to move forward . . . opening my soul to the world, even if it meant to just one person. People often talk about their "bucket list." My life with John had been full, with family, friends, pets, travels, some accomplishments, and all the joys and sorrows that life brought. We had lived and loved and I truly felt that nothing was left undone . . . except for the book. It is today my privilege to be sharing it with you.

As the years passed, indecisions and doubts sometimes cluttered my vision on the course my journey was taking me. Invariably, at those times, 11:11 has been, and continues to be, a constant reminder of the short distance between our two Worlds. The energy that it brings, although short-lived, lets me know that I am exactly where I am supposed to be. In that moment, there is always peace and freedom.

A bright cardinal often perches himself on the ring where the bird feeder is still suspended and looks toward the window, where so much of my journey revealed itself.

In the last few years, he has showed up even in the summer months, often when my soul is searching for remnants of what was, and it always brings me joy. A few years ago, while I was on the phone with our daughter Jessica, the bright red cardinal appeared in the window. At that same moment, she exclaimed "Mom, dad's here. . . ." A bright red cardinal had just landed on the window sill of her office located on the second floor of a building in Toledo, fifty miles away.

For many years, on the anniversary of John's passing, I would place a red rose on each site where "the ceremony of the burial of the ashes" took place. The ritual doesn't happen consistently anymore. It has become entwined with the mélange of emotions embedded deeply in the fibers of my being.

The outdoors continues to be a source of solace and peace. Unsettled feelings always seem to get resolved as I go for walks in the familiar woods that surround me, with my dog Gabriel. So much beauty and so many lessons on living . . . like the small, bright, colorful butterfly that dances around us as we walk in the brisk air of early spring, much too early for butterflies to have made the journey; like the tiny periwinkle wild flower standing alone in the middle of the path, being what it is meant to be—hearty and beautiful—in spite of the tall weeds surrounding it; like the dead trees that still stand tall, their branches sustaining new life, as moss and vines grow on their bare branches; like the wild flowers decorating the fields in the early spring, only to resurface in greater number in the middle of summer after being mowed to the ground, which makes the land look lifeless and desolate; like the leaves lining the path in the fall—though fallen from their source of life, the sound of their crackling under foot and the mesmerizing play of colors under the sun brings added life to an ordinary and familiar experience; like the autumn foliage along the highways, resonating in my soul like a chorus singing a song of joy to the Divine; like the carefree deer gallivanting through the snow-covered fields; like. . . .

So many lessons in living, being, waiting, dying, and staying alive. . . . It always brings me back to the moment and I am grateful for all of it.

As years went by, my affinity to the Other Side expanded in a way that I never would have expected. I remember when someone I had been very close to through my work stood by my dining room table, while I was hearing of her death on the phone. My younger brother who died a few years earlier has made his presence known on several occasions, always when I wished to quiet my mind as the sound of people buzzed around me. Always, peace settles in my mind and soul. He had visited me with his daughter the year before he passed away, and my niece who loves to make jewelry had given me a chain with a black butterfly hanging on it. I thought it was odd . . . I had never seen a black butterfly. The summer after his death, a black butterfly danced around me as I walked in the woods. Incredible!

Shortly after my dear friend who was like a sister to me passed away, I was walking the path that we had often walked together with my dog, Gabriel, when a strong, sweet fragrance filled the air. I got closer to the only patch of wild flowers near us, enthralled by the sweetness emanating from flowers that had never had a scent in all the years. . . . *Was this real?* I wondered as I started walking away. I had to be sure, so I retraced my steps and to my amazement, I smelled once again the indubitable fragrance from those flowers. Joy welled up inside my being and my step felt lighter as I walked the familiar path. I walked back with anticipation only to find the wild flowers just the way they had always been. No scent. To this day, every time I walk by the patch of flowers, I am reminded of a special gift from a special friend and I am forever grateful for her friendship.

I still sit by the window, but time matters now . . . life is full with family, friends, physical activities, travels, quiet time, a Twelve Steps support group that gave me a new lease on life decades ago, and writing. There was a first book inspired by an incident that happened in my early years of marriage to John. On a very ordinary morning, as I walked into the living room, I was startled by the reflection looking back at me from the mirrored wall in the room. My eyes were fixed on an enormous, black, ominous bubble in the center of my being. I had to know. . . .

Years later, when it was close to completion, the manuscript vanished as I pressed a wrong key on my old computer. I started writing again in 2002, the year before John crossed over. I had not looked at it since. Today, the book seems even more relevant as I write. . . .

Recently, the PBS TV Station had a documentary on the life of John Denver. I had just put some rhubarb in a pot on the stove with a little water and plenty of sugar when John Denver began singing "Annie's Song." That many years later, the song reminded me how full life was with Johnny at my side. Tears flowing softly, I let the words penetrate my entire being until the sweet, burnt smell on the stove brought me back to reality.

Last week, as I sat by the window, quiet and pensive, the bright red cardinal came very close and danced, wings fluttering freely from one side of the window to the other. A moment to behold! He then flew away only to return twice and repeat the dance all over again. It has been years since the encounters with the butterflies. Even during a visit to a butterfly garden in Cincinnati, where butterflies landed on children and adults alike, not one landed on me, no matter how I tried to reach out. A few days ago, as I sat quietly on the back patio, a bright, colorful Monarch landed on my chest and made its way to my right arm, touching my skin lightly, up and down, until it flew away—a joy-filled encounter.

Every morning, I look forward to the rushed sound of hummingbirds, wings beating rapidly as they playfully land on the yellow flower on the feeder and drink of the "nectar of the gods." Then there are the rabbits—mom, dad, and babies—running and feasting all through the yard, and all the small creatures that make life colorful and joyous and keep me centered in the moment . . . these are the things that fill my heart with love and gratitude . . . the simple things that were so meaningful in our lives.

"Mom, that's the way we lived," Jessica often reminds me. I always say, "Thank you for the joy," to God and to John. As I write this the boys are in their teenage years. Ian has completed his first year of college and Owen will be a senior in high school. To this day, neither one of them has ever ended a phone conversation or a text message without the words "Je t'aime." And, without fail, this little French phrase feels like a soft feather caressing my heart. What a gift!

The ring that hung on the chain around my neck for so many years has now become part of a beautiful piece of jewelry, as both of our wedding rings were cut to form four entangled rings with the diamond in the middle—a perfect symbol of eternal love.

Through the years, peace has become a welcome companion for most of my days as the "letting go" has finally let go. . . . It feels almost natural to think of the two of us as, "You with me the way you are and me with you the way I am." How grateful I am for the love that lives on. It has been a full, heartbreaking, joyful, challenging, and rewarding journey and I am grateful for all of it. I have no regrets. This is my journey and I wouldn't change a thing.

Johnny and me in Montreal, 2000, our last trip to Quebec

Made in the USA
Monee, IL
19 September 2020

42517621R00105